Singapore and Asia in a Globalized World

Contemporary Economic Issues and Policies

Singapore and Asia in a Globalized World

Contemporary Economic Issues and Policies

Editors

Chia Wai Mun

Sng Hui Ying

School of Humanities & Social Sciences,
Nanyang Technological University, Singapore

World Scientific

NEW JERSEY • LONDON • SINGAPORE • BEIJING • SHANGHAI • HONG KONG • TAIPEI • CHENNAI

Published by

World Scientific Publishing Co. Pte. Ltd.
5 Toh Tuck Link, Singapore 596224
USA office: 27 Warren Street, Suite 401-402, Hackensack, NJ 07601
UK office: 57 Shelton Street, Covent Garden, London WC2H 9HE

British Library Cataloguing-in-Publication Data
A catalogue record for this book is available from the British Library.

SINGAPORE AND ASIA IN A GLOBALIZED WORLD
Contemporary Economic Issues and Policies

ISBN-13 978-981-281-557-6
ISBN-10 981-281-557-0

Typeset by Stallion Press
Email: enquiries@stallionpress.com

Printed in Singapore by Mainland Press Pte Ltd.

Foreword

Economics is a very important and useful subject. These words, coming from an economist, would probably invite skepticism from people of other disciplines. However, being an educator for close to half a century, I would say from my teaching experience that fundamental training in Economics allows our students to think more critically and enables them to better understand world economic and world financial policies, problems and issues. The latter, in particular, is increasingly important in view of the current turmoil in the global economy.

Since 2006, the Division of Economics of Nanyang Technological University (NTU) has been working with the Ministry of Education (MOE) to organize economic seminars for Junior Colleges (JCs) students and teachers every year. The objectives are to present to our youngsters and their teachers contemporary economic issues and public policies in Singapore as well as the region. We also aim to introduce the wide-ranging fields of the study of economics to the students. These seminars have been very well-received by the JCs students and teachers, with more than 1,000 participants attending the seminars each year.

This year, the NTU-MOE Seminars were held in March 2008. The response was overwhelming, and there is currently a plan to double the capacity of subsequent seminars. There are also interests from the polytechnics to participate in the subsequent seminars. The NTU-MOE Seminars 2008 had put together a list of distinguished and proficient speakers covering a wide range of economic issues that are integral to the Singapore economy. I am very glad that World Scientific Publishing Company has decided to publish these papers that were presented during the NTU-MOE Seminars 2008, so as to increase the accessibility of these papers.

There are a total of 13 papers in this book. Issues discussed and reviewed include healthcare, social security, monetary policy, economic transformation, globalization, sub-prime crisis and Asian economic integration. I believe that readers of this book, would benefit from having a better understanding of the world economic and world financial policies, problems and issues as well as those facing Singapore and the region.

April 2008

LIM Chong Yah
Albert Winsemius Chair Professor of Economics
Director of Economic Growth Centre
Division of Economics
School of Humanities and Social Sciences
Nanyang Technological University

Contents

Part I

Public Policies and Economic Issues of Singapore

Chapter

1

Transformation in the Singapore Economy: Course and Causes*

Lim Chong Yah†

Has there been an economic miracle in Singapore? How do we measure this miracle? Is it measurable? How and why has this miracle taken place in Singapore for the last 43 years after Independence in 1965? What structural changes have taken place in the economy? What special institutions have been created to engineer this transformation? What is the critical role of the State in this transformation process, particularly in terms of its effects on investment in human capital, physical capital and social capital? The focus of this chapter is on the course and causes of the rapid transformation in income and wealth creation, with the support of some interesting stylized facts and photographs since Independence in 1965 through 2008.

---

* Lecture given at the NTU-MOE Seminar 2008 at NTU on 8th March 2008. It is an updated and revised version of the original lecture under the title: *"The Singapore Economy: The Right Options"* given at the Singapore Soka Association Youth Peace Lecture in April 2007.

† The views expressed herein are his personal views. The author wishes to thank his Research Assistant, Ms Sarah Chan, for updating the statistics in this Chapter.

THE ECONOMIC MIRACLE

Per Capital GDP Growth

(a) In US Dollar

In 1965, when Singapore became a fully independent Republic, the per capita GDP was typical of that of developing countries at US$512 per annum. Today, 43 years later, as per 2007 figures, the per capita GDP went up by 63.7 times to US$32,624 per annum, typical of that of the First World. These figures are in nominal US dollars.

(b) In Singapore Dollar

Because of the secular appreciation of the Singapore dollar *vis-a-vis* the US dollar between 1965 and 2007, in Singapore dollar terms, the nominal per capita GDP went up from S$1,567 in 1965 to S$49,182 in 2007, a reduced increase of 31.4 times as against 63.7 times in US dollar terms.

Growth in GDP Sizes

Below are two figures showing the size of the economy in 1965 compare to its size today, one in real and the other in nominal terms.

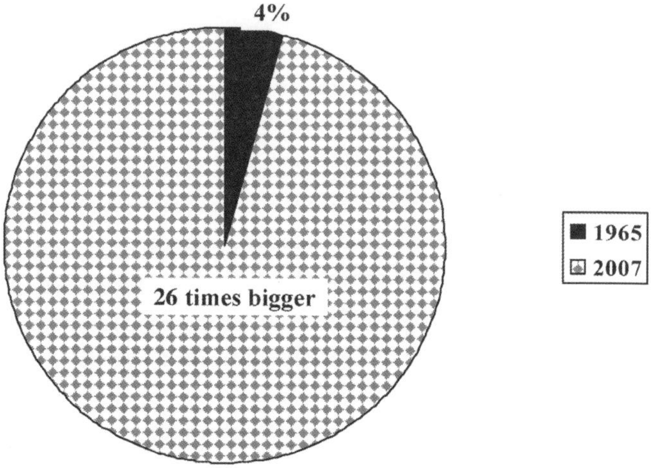

Figure 1: Metamorphosis in real GDP sizes (S$)

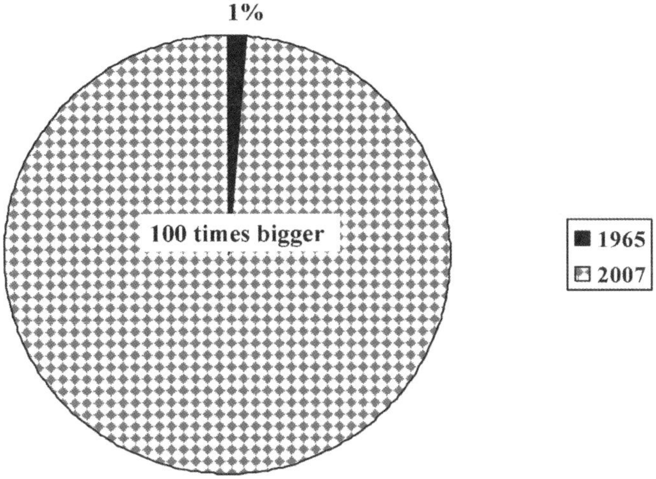

Figure 2: Metamorphosis in nominal GDP sizes (S$)

Of note is that Singapore's real GDP in 1965 was only 4% of today's GDP. When nominal GDP figures are compared, in 1965, it was only 1% of the present GDP.

Growth in Real GDP Rates

In terms of long-term real growth rate, the average per annum was 7.4% in US dollars and 5.6% in Singapore dollars. These are spectacular average compound real per capita growth rates over a period of 43 years. The speed of growth in Singapore has been about 3 to 4 times the growth rate of developed economies, with the steady and rapid convergence with the developed economies over time. The year to year real growth rates from 1961 through 2007 are given in the table below.

Note the gyrations in real growth rates over time, with a low of −1.4% in 1985 to a high of 13.7% in 1970. The average compound growth rate for 43 years is 8.1%.

Standards of Living

As shown in Fig. 3, Singapore's real per capita GDP grew from S$4,668 in 1965 to S$48,158 in 2007 i.e., an increase of 10.3 times. In other

Table 1: Singapore's Real GDP Growth Rates, 2000 Market Prices (1961–2007)

Year	Growth	Year	Growth	Year	Growth	Year	Growth	Year	Growth
1961	8.0	1971	12.0	1981	9.7	1991	6.6	2001	–2.4
1962	7.0	1972	13.4	1982	7.1	1992	6.3	2002	4.2
1963	9.9	1973	11.1	1983	8.5	1993	11.7	2003	3.1
1964	–3.8	1974	6.1	1984	8.3	1994	11.6	2004	8.8
1965	7.5	1975	4.1	1985	–1.4	1995	8.1	2005	6.6
1966	10.8	1976	7.1	1986	2.1	1996	7.8	2006	7.9
1967	12.2	1977	7.8	1987	9.8	1997	8.3	2007	7.7
1968	13.6	1978	8.5	1988	11.5	1998	–1.4	—	—
1969	13.6	1979	9.4	1989	10.0	1999	7.2	—	—
1970	13.7	1980	9.7	1990	9.2	2000	10.1	—	—
Average	9.3	Average	8.9	Average	7.5	Average	7.6	Average	5.1

Source: www.singstat.gov.sg

Note: 1965–2007 = 8.1%

World Average (1980–1999) = 2.8% (*own estimate*)

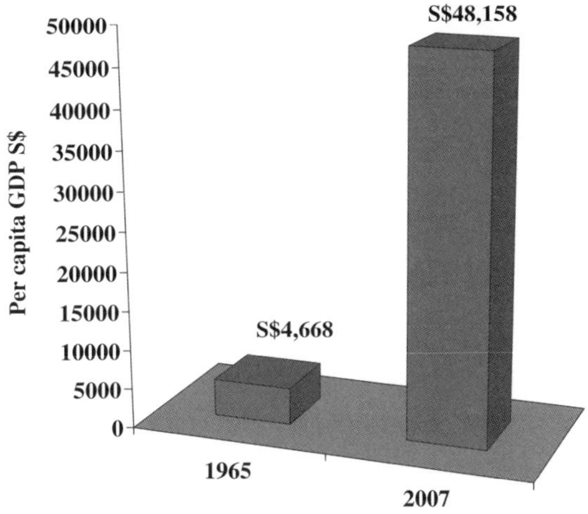

Note: Real capita GDP increased by 10.3 times.

Figure 3: Singapore's real per capita GDP in S$

words, deflating for inflation rates to real terms, *the general standards of living in Singapore increased by about 10 times between 1965 and 2007.* This is an average figure. It roughly means that half of the families in Singapore had their standards of living raised by more than 10 times and the other half by less than 10 times, between 1965 and 2007.

Employment Creation

Concomitant with the spectacular GDP expansion, about 2 million new jobs have been added to the economy by 2007, when compared to 1965. Besides, the jobs today fetch higher pay than in 1965; some are more than 10 times higher today and some less than 10 times. There has been a spectacular increase in the variety and range of jobs available in 2008, when compared to 1965. There is a very close correlation between job creation and GDP expansion.

An Economic Miracle

By the growth measures mentioned above, the economic transformation in Singapore between 1965 and 2007 was remarkable, extraordinary, and very impressive by any standard, whether it be inter-temporal or international.

How did this extra-ordinary income and wealth creation after Independence in 1965 come about? This is considered, by the World Bank, as an economic miracle.

As a result of this economic metamorphosis, the red-spot on the map called Singapore, now has a GDP in US dollar terms that is surprisingly 87% bigger than five of our rapidly growing beloved neighbors, and some much bigger neighbors, namely Vietnam, Myanmar, Cambodia, and Laos combined. Singapore's total GDP is US$125.3 billion.[1] The combined GDP of the four important neighboring countries mentioned above is US$67.0 billion.[1] This is an unbelievable feat Singapore has accomplished. Its transformation may be compared to a caterpillar metamorphosing into a butterfly, or as per the S Curve Theory, from a turtle economy to an elephant economy, a nascent elephant economy (Lim, 2004) or, in more common parlance, from the Third World to the First.

STRUCTURAL TRANSFORMATION

Structurally, the economy was heavily dependent on two pillars at the time of Independence: the entrepot trade of primary products, principally of rubber and tin; as a British military base, East of Suez. After Independence, outward-looking industrialization was bud-grafted into the old economic framework. As a part of the outward-looking industrialization process, Singapore successfully established itself as an important oil-refinery center; as a center for electronic and pharmaceutic products and a center for maritime products such as oil-rigs. Rapid industrialization was soon to be accompanied by three other important developments: (1) Singapore as an international transportation and logistic hub; (2) as a financial entrepot; and (3) as a center for international tourism. Later, two more pillars were added: (1) Singapore as a regional educational center and (2) as a regional center for health care and medical services. The last five

[1] As per 2006 statistics.

pillars are still, in varying degrees, in the rapid expansion phase, whilst outward-looking industrialization and the old entrepot trade underwent and still continue to go through important restructuring and upgrading process.

In entrepot trade, rubber and tin faded into the horizon, to be substituted by petrol-chemicals, electronics, pharmaceuticals, and other manufactured goods.

In manufacturing, as in other sectors, the restructuring process also took the form of more higher valued-added goods in place of labor-intensive, low value-added products. For example, Singapore today builds and exports as much as 75% of the oil-rigs in the world, whereas in the beginning of the industrialization process, low-end and low-valued added consumer goods like ordinary soaps, soap powder, mosquito coils, rubber slippers, toothbrushes, toothpastes, and saw-milling were the important job-providers.

On tourism, at the commencement of the rapid development process, the pessimism for development was so great that it was rightly thought that only drunken sailors would visit Singapore as tourists, contrasting with some 10 million international visitors a year today. With the introduction of the two integrated international resorts, the numbers are expected to show further increases.

On the financial side, because of our political and social instability at that time, there was more fear of money outflow than money inflow as is happening today. As it is, Singapore's financial center today can boast of numerous world-class banks and other world-class financial institutions. Foreign exchange transactions alone in a day amount to some US$159 billion and a monthly turnover of US$3.3 trillion.

Of course, the growth of Singapore as a high value-added, outward-looking manufacturing base, an international tourism hub, a financial emporium, a regional educational center, a regional health-care center, and a super trading emporium must go hand in hand with Singapore emerging as an international shipping center as well as an international aviation center. The equally rapid upgrading in domestic transportation, including the MRT, and communications including computer suaveness and ubiquitous usage, are all integral

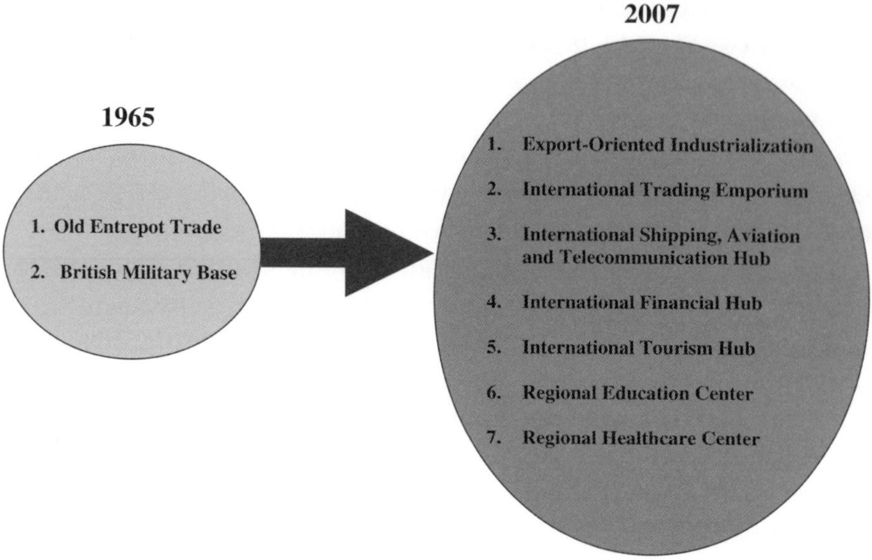

Figure 4: Economic structural transformation

parts of the overall economic transformation process. Each development builds on the other developments in a circular cumulative upward surge.

Singapore's miraculous structural transformation is shown in Fig. 4.

In other words, Singapore's overall economic pie expanded in real GDP terms by an average compound rate of 8.1% per year for the last 43 years. This is a very impressive, record-breaking achievement by any standard. More than that, Singapore's rapid rate of growth in income and wealth has been achieved with price stability, huge accumulation of foreign exchange reserves, a stable and strong Singapore dollar, full employment for most of the 43 years, a very high savings function and the most enviable balance of payments surpluses. Singapore's unemployment rate is 2.7%, one of the very lowest in the world. Germany, for example, which is the biggest economy and one of the most dynamic countries in Europe, has an unemployment rate of 8.1% and France also has an unemployment rate of 8.1%. Singapore has been transformed from a low value-added, labor intensive old economy to a much higher value-added, knowledge-based and technology-based new economy.

METAMORPHOSIS IN EXTERNAL BALANCE

Some countries, including the USA, have recently achieved a very high standard of living partly through the accumulation of foreign debts. This is not the case in Singapore. Singapore has become very much a creditor nation, than a debtor country. Again, some countries, including the USA, have achieved a very high standard of living but have serious balance of payments deficit. Again this is not the case in Singapore. Singapore has one of the highest balance of payments surpluses on current account in the world, reaching 25.5% of GDP in 2007. Incidentally, not many of us are aware that from 1965 up to 1987, Singapore normally ran a sizable balance of payments deficit on current account, culminating at 32.2% of GDP in 1971.

METAMORPHOSIS IN SAVINGS FUNCTION

Singapore has one of the highest savings rates in the world, constituting 46.3% of GDP in 2006. However, not many of us are aware that at one time, Singapore had a negative savings function. In 1960, for example, our savings rate was minus 2.4% of GDP. At times, I come across the claim that Singapore has a high average and marginal propensity to save, because of its compulsory savings system under its very important CPF scheme. This claim is erroneous. It is just another statistical fallacy. CPF compulsory savings constitute only 11% of GDP. The rest, the other savings, constitute 89% of GDP. The other savings take the form of the enviable private sector company surpluses, public sector surpluses, GLC surpluses, and surpluses in individual and household accounts (Hsieh, 2002). Incidentally, it is this very high accumulation of savings that has enabled the Singapore Government to contribute importantly to global welfare by lending to world famous financial institutions caught in the prevailing sub-prime crisis. These world famous financial institutions in difficulty include UBS, the Citigroup and Merrill Lynch.

GROWTH ACCOUNTING

Earlier, we mentioned that about 2 million new jobs were added to the economy between 1965 and 2007. However, this impressive expansion in labor input may reflect only quantitative expansion. The quantitative expansion includes more housewives going out to work and more foreign workers being employed. There was, however, important qualitative expansion as well, not apparent from the figures. According to my own research estimate, 78% of Singapore's miraculous economic expansion could be attributed to increase in labor productivity and only 22% to the increase in labor input (Lim and Lee, 2002).

Gauti Eggertsson of the IMF, who made a special study on Singapore's growth prospects, reported in 2004 that, between 1990 and 2003, the Total Factor Productivity (TFP) accounted for 26% of the actual growth of GDP in Singapore, compared with the corresponding average of 20% for the Industrial Countries. The rest of the growth in Singapore was contributed by Labor (19%), Capital (41%) and Education (13%) (Eggertsson, 2004; Ghesquiere, 2007). Dr Eggertsson's figures and Professor Hsieh's seminal research paper (Hsieh, 2002) both contradict earlier publications of very negligible or no TFP growth for Singapore (Lall *et al.*, 1996).

VISUAL GLIMPSES

We are living in an audio-visual age. I have thus far only share with you some important macro-economic statistics, to show the reality and extent of our economic transformation. Perhaps now, I should share with you some photographs on a few other facets of the transformation.

Exhibit 1 shows small attap huts before transformation. There was no electricity or potable water supply. Toilet facilities are best left undescribed.

Exhibit 2 shows Singaporeans shifting from their attap houses to HDB flats, carrying all their precious belongings along.

Exhibit 1: How Singaporeans lived — A glimpse (*before transformation*)

Source: National Archives.

Exhibit 2: Singaporeans on the move to better dwelling places (*Note the furniture, the mud road and the debris before transformation*)

Source: National Archives.

Exhibit 3 shows, by way of contrast, the modern public housing in Singapore. Incidentally, today most Singaporeans, more than 90%, own their own homes. There are no more frightening ubiquitous slums that existed before. Shenton Way, for example, was a slum area. Today, it is one of the most expensive pieces of real estate in Southeast Asia.

Exhibit 4 shows traffic congestion by small bump-boats *(tongkangs)*, at the mouth of the Singapore River.

Exhibit 5 shows coolies laboring hard for a living, transporting gunny-sacks of rice. This was the usual sight at the mouth of the Singapore River. Incidentally, I can still recall, that I had the honor and privilege of supervising a BA Hons economic thesis on this tongkang trade and tongkang workers of one student who later became a famous and well-accomplished Permanent Secretary in Singapore.

Exhibits 6 & 7 show the metamorphosis in the landscape and skyline at the mouth of the Singapore River. Singapore's port, has become one of the busiest and biggest in the world, certainly

Exhibit 3: Present public housing in Singapore

Source: Postcard, Photo by R. Ian Lloyd.

Exhibit 4: Congestion at Singapore river (*before transformation*)

Source: National Archives.

Exhibit 5: Coolie-dependent river transport system (*before transformation*)

Source: National Archives.

Exhibit 6: Present landscape at Singapore river

Source: National Archives.

Exhibit 7: Another snapshot just outside Singapore river

Source: *The Business Times*, 10 April 2007.

the most important container port in the world. Incidentally, half of the world's oil, a third of the world's foreign trade and over 50,000 ocean-going ships per year use the narrow Straits of Singapore today.

THREE CRITICAL OPTIONS

What basic policy alternatives have Singapore adopted to enhance its international competitiveness? What basic policy options have Singapore pursued to bring about the economic transformation miracle? These two closely related questions will be briefly discussed under three broad headings:

(1) the option for a market-oriented, outward-looking economic policy;
(2) the option for the most impressive investment in physical capital, human capital and social capital; and
(3) the most important one, the option for and the active promotion of an able, stable, people-oriented, development-oriented, corruption-free, innovative Government and bureaucracy.

(1) Market-Orientation

A market-oriented outward-looking policy is critical for Singapore's transformation, if the alternative is a command or a completely state-managed economy or economic autarky. Market orientation ensures the optimum use of scarce resources in the production and exchange of goods and services. Outward-lookingness ensures Singapore operates and competes in the global environment. The price mechanism, or the invisible hand, equilibrates supply and demand. Production is for the market, global market. Price is determined by supply and demand. High prices are signals of shortages, and low prices are signals of over-supply.

Thus, Singapore's enormous external visible trade is surprisingly even much higher, some 88% higher, than that of all the countries in the Indian Sub-Continent combined. This huge complex multi-lateral trading system cannot take place and could not have taken place without the invisible hand and the outward-orientation of the economy. External trade has been handled almost exclusively by the private sector. Even when only Singapore's domestic exports are considered, surprisingly, they still exceed the gross exports of the important countries in the vast fast-expanding Indian Sub-Continent combined. Incidentally, trade, including international trade, takes place on a willing-buyer and willing-seller basis, and both parties benefit in the exchange. International trade, both visible and invisible trade, reflects one of Singapore's most important roles in the regional and global economy. Nor could the other important facets of the Singaporean economy develop without the whole-hearted commitment in the pursuit of the outward-looking, and market-orientation policy and strategy.

The ubiquitous Government-linked Corporations (GLCs) could not have played such a critical role in Singapore's economic transformation process, had they remained purely as Government Departments or Statutory Boards. The Singapore Government-created GLCs are subject to the economic calculus of market forces, and guided by the invisible hand. Like other private sector corporations, they operate under the Companies Act and the Singapore Exchange Listing Rules, including having their own independent board of directors, internal and external audit checking system, own nomination, remuneration and audit committees. The GLCs also report directly to their shareholders with quarterly, half-yearly and yearly reports published for all to see and evaluate. They too pay the usual company taxes and their employees, the usual personal income tax and other taxes. Besides, the anxiety of GLCs to relocate to other countries in an economic downturn is zero. Their assets to the extent that their shares are state-owned, continue to belong to the State, or Singaporeans. Also, Singaporeans and others are free to own their shares, and prosper with the GLCs, as they fly high in the economic firmament in and outside Singapore.

The virtues of the GLCs are deliberately paraded because, they are Singapore-created growth agencies and are often denigrated by some laisser-fairists both inside and outside Singapore. The IMF, for example, wants to know more about the GLCs in Singapore. They commissioned two economists to investigate and report on them. The two economists express the view that GLCs in Singapore are very successful, viable, profit-making commercial organizations, without the need for State subsidy for their operation and success. They vindicated our GLCs as very successful market-oriented state capitalism (Ramirez and Tan, 2003). Incidentally, GLCs include listed iconic-companies like SIA, SINGTEL, DBS, NOL, Keppel Corporation, Sembawang Corporation, Keppel Land, Capital Land, and the unlisted one, PSA. Indeed, many GLCs qualify, from the extent of their regional and global operations, as Singapore's MNCs. SIA, SINGTEL, Keppel Corporation, Sembawang Corporation, and ST Engineering are cases in point.

Similarly, without market-orientation and outward-orientation, foreign MNCs, which also play a critical role in Singapore's rapid transformation, particularly in the industrial sector, would not have a place in the Singapore economy. In short, without outward-looking market-orientation, neither the foreign MNCs nor the home-grown GLCs could have flourished. Singapore's domestic market is small. That however, can also become an asset. Any company established in Singapore has to face the full blast of international competition straight away. SIA, a GLC, is often cited as an example. Internal commercial flight by high-speed jet commercial planes such as from Changi to Tuas is not economical, even if technically possible. Keppel FELS and Sembawang Marine, both GLCs, for example, build, *inter-alia*, oil rigs for exports only; there being no oil wells in Singapore for oil rigs.

(2) Investment, Investment and Investment

The economic system needs a progressive increase in investment: human capital investment, physical capital investment and social capital investment. The need for appropriate physical capital investment is well-known, including in the supporting public sector, such as the MRT, the road system, the seaports and the airports. The need for human capital investment is less obvious, partly because of the longer gestation period required. But for sustained and sustainable development, human capital investment is a *sine qua non* to success. More than that, its appropriate human capital investment mix is also critical. Singapore has done very well indeed both in physical capital investment and in human capital investment both in quantity as well as in quality and in the capital mix. Together, the physical and human capital investments have enabled the transformation, or the metamorphosis, in Singapore to take place.

More investment means more job opportunities, more income and more savings. They in turn bring in more investments and more employment creation in an upward circular cumulative causation process.

Quantitatively, in 1965, the total value of Singapore's capital stock is estimated by Dr Sng Hui Ying, when she was my Ph.D student, as S$21 billion. Singapore's capital stock went up to S$795 billion by 2004 (Sng, 2007). The enormous increase in capital input explains the enormous increase in income output. Investment can in turn be decomposed into domestic private investment, foreign direct investment (FDI) and public investment. All three parameters have gone up by leaps and bounds. All three, particularly domestic private investment and foreign investment, have reacted to the outward-looking, market-oriented policy and strategy in Singapore.

Singapore's human capital stock has also metamorphosed. The very narrow domestic talent pyramid at the apex has also become very much broader, with about 70% of the school cohorts opting for higher education today, compared to 6% in 1965.

Social capital here refers to institutional building, such as the promotion of ethnic harmony, religious respect, tripartism among the unions, the employers and the Government, and the common pursuit of meritocracy. Together, they contribute critically to the building of a favorable economic climate for investment to flourish. One should quickly add that a good investment climate also includes fundamental prerequisites like the rule of law, equal protection before the law, protection of property rights and an effective, impartial and non-corrupt judicial system.

Two other important policy options that have important growth-enhancing and growth-promoting side effects need to be mentioned here: (1) the institution of national service following Independence. If a small, new nation, a city state, is not prepared to defend itself, defend its newly-won sovereignty, its people and its property, investor confidence in that nation will decline, particularly in a not-that-stable Southeast Asian political environment. (2) the choice of using English as the working language in administration, in the courts and in institutions of learning. The wide-spread mastery of the English language gives Singapore and Singaporeans an important edge in the globalised world; in trade, commerce, industry, knowledge acquisition and global social connectivity. Bilingualism, however, gives us an important cultural ballast, particularly as an Asian nation in Asia.

(3) Good Public Governance

Earlier, we spoke of the importance of the invisible hand in the transformation process. Now, we should speak of the equal importance of a good supporting visible hand. If the two hands clap in unison, they produce effective joyful sound. Alone, they are useless. The ying and the yang must not just be side by side. They must be like opposites that complement. They must support each other in a symbiotic relationship. In Singapore, both hands work together. Both ying and yang complement, each re-enforcing the other in a virtuous cycle of job creation, poverty eradication and more and greater affluence. Working together, the economy surges forward. The nature, the extent, and above all, the quality of State intervention, is critical. Markets are made for man and not man for the markets. A market-only policy can often create more problems than what a modern civilized society can handle. Market failures and market imperfections often justify State interventions and State initiatives.

At the apex of the human determinants of development is the Government and its accompanying and supporting bureaucracy. Government decides on the policy options, whether to have MNCs, GLCs, government agencies like EDB, NWC, SDF, HDB, and CPF, free trade, outward-looking market orientation, meritocracy, employment creation, or none of these. It is also the Government that decides on the type of monetary system, the exchange rate regime, the fiscal policy, the meritocratic practice, the welfare and workforce system.

It is the Government that decides on all important creations and operations of the Government of Singapore Investment Corporation Pte Ltd (GIC) and the Temasek Holdings (Private) Limited. They are today referred to as sovereign wealth funds (SWFs). Because of the success of our GLC, China has also set up a similar body called Chinese Investment Corporation (CIC). If the Chinese character for human, "人", can be used as an analogy, Government is at the apex or head, without which there is no functioning society, like a human without a head. The society could function only like a headless chicken, and the headless chicken could go nowhere, maybe round and round before collapse. Thus, the aptitude and attitude of the Government, particularly its integrity and management ability, is critical in the transformation process. A corrupt and incompetent Government would be unable to lead the economy out of poverty and low-level equilibrium trap. Some years ago, going against the trend in economic literature, in a book called Development and Underdevelopment, I postulated that "*Government, good Government often holds the key to rapid economic development*", particularly in developing economies (Lim, 1991). Many, many years later, I still hold firmly to the same view. The world, in particular the World Bank, appears to increasingly share this perception and approach.

In other words, a stable, able and development-oriented Government is critical in the rapid developmental process. However, the people, particularly the businessmen, merchants, industrialists, entrepreneurs, unions, and the workers too each have their important role to play in the process of economic upliftment. Nonetheless, labor and capital must work together not against, their legitimate elected Government to create the economic miracle. In Singapore, this togetherness among the three social partners is often referred to as tripartisim. This tripartite symbiotic relationship, partnership, is critical to the metamorphosis of the Singapore economy from Third World to First, from a basket-case to a show-case state, from a per capita income of US$512 per annum in 1965 to US$32,624 per annum in 2007, and from the old economy to the new economy.

To conclude, Singapore has been succeeding miraculously against all odds for the last 43 years since Independence, because throughout the 43 years Singapore has had and is still having an able, stable, non-corrupt, development-oriented Government, and has been choosing the road of an outward-looking, market-based, meritocratic economy and society, besides being populated with a hard-working, pragmatic and achievement-oriented people in a strategic location in South-East Asia and in the world.

END NOTES

Lim, CY (1991). *Development and Underdevelopment*. Singapore: Longman Publications.

Lall, Tan and Chew (1996). Total Factor Productivity Growth Experience of Singapore: An Interpretive Survey. In *Economic Policy Management in Singapore*, Lim CY (ed.). Singapore: Addison-Wesley.

Hsieh, C-T (2002). What explains the industrial revolution in East Asia? Evidence from the factor markets. *The American Economic Review* 92(3), pp. 502–526.

Lim, CY and CT Lee (2002). An examination of labor productivity growth and structural changes in the Singapore labor force. *Asian Economic Journal* 16(3), pp. 267–283.

Ramirez, CD and LH Tan (2003). *Singapore, Inc. versus the private sector: Are Government-linked companies different?* IMF Working Paper No. 03/156.

Lim, CY (2004). Southeast Asia: The Long Road Ahead, 2nd Ed. Singapore: World Scientific.

Eggertsson, G (2004). *Medium-Term Growth Prospects*, Singapore: Selected Issues, IMF Staff Country Report No. 04/103.

Ghesquiere, H (2007). Singapore's Success: Engineering Economic Growth. Singapore: Thomson.

Sng, HY (2007). *Economic Growth and Transition: Econometric Analysis of Lim's S-Curve Hypothesis*. Unpublished PhD Thesis, Nanyang Technological University.

Chapter

2

Innovation, Markets and Economic Growth: A Symbiosis

Lam Chuan Leong

Innovation is now accepted by economists as essential to economic growth. It is therefore very important to understand what factors foster the rate of innovation and sustain it.

A DETAILED LOOK AT INNOVATION

O-Type Innovation and V-Type Innovation

Innovation may be classified into two types: O-type and V-type innovation. O-type innovation is aimed at refining existing products or ideas through the application of codified knowledge. The long educational and schooling process of humans is intended to equip them to acquire and apply codified knowledge to undertake O-type innovation. Examples of this are studies in engineering, medicine, or any other professional courses.

In contrast, V-type innovation is a creative process, aimed at creating new products, inventions and ideas, not known before. These innovations are not arrived at, through a systematic rational process using known scientific or social "laws". Much of this innovation is a process of an association of ideas, connecting different ideas to come up with a new one. For e.g., the Walkman is a V-type innovation as defined here. It is the idea of combining a sound reproduction system with the idea of portability. Adding the idea of a small sound production apparatus to the idea of small earphones led to the great invention of the Walkman. This idea has become so popular that its descendants today in the form of the MP3 players are widely used.

The Innovation Cycle and Economic Growth

O-type innovation needs V-type innovation to supply new product ideas to improve upon. V-type innovations need a lot of work by O-type innovation, to make the initial product better appealing to the mass market. V- and O-type innovations therefore work in tandem to create "The Innovation Cycle" (see Fig. 1) to bring about the great variety of products that define the standard of living in the modern economy. History shows that economic growth and prosperity are strongest during those periods when there is a surge of new ideas and inventions brought about by innovation, e.g., the growth cycles following the invention of the steam engine, the motor car, the use of

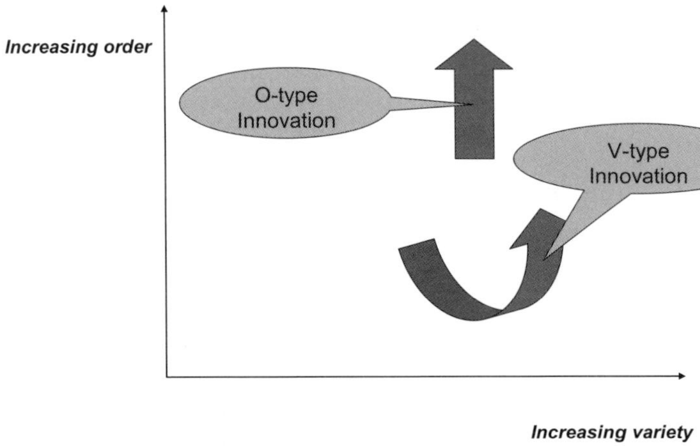

Figure 1: The innovation cycle

electric power, and the railroads. Hence the innovation cycle can be considered one of the engines for economic growth.

INNOVATION AND MARKETS — A SYMBIOSIS

A new idea is of no use unless the invention that follows from it can be turned into a product and brought to the market. Many factors can impede this process and make a country less innovative than it should be. On the other hand, economic policies and practices are in a position to improve the conditions under which innovation has a better chance of success. The factors that improve the chances of success of innovations can be grouped under 4 headings:

- Free diffusion of information and knowledge;
- Free market entry and exit;
- An *ex-poste* market "selection system"; and
- Sustaining reward system.

Free Diffusion of Information and Diffusion of Knowledge

A free flow and diffusion of information is critical to innovation. Cut off from previous knowledge, even great geniuses would have to re-invent the wheel. The supply of new ideas would therefore be very slow. One reason for the rapid rise in innovation in the last two centuries is the tremendous improvements in transportation and communications. During the last 20 years, the advent of information technology and the Internet have enabled information to be diffused widely and at very low cost. This has tremendously accelerated the pace of change and innovation.

Free Market Entry and Exit

The cost and difficulty of setting up companies vary from country to country. Those countries, like Singapore, which make it easy for people to start businesses and have fewer rules restricting their behavior, will favor innovators because, it would be easier for them to set up a business entity to commercialize their inventions. India is an example of a country with an onerous licencing regime and restrictive regulations that impede the setting up of businesses and thus reduces the rate of innovation and its commercialization. Consequently, it grows possibly at a lower rate than its potential (William *et al.*, 2007). China during its days of central planning did not allow private business startups. Commercialization of innovation was almost non-existent and the economic growth was retarded. For innovation to flourish, freedom from distortions, restrictions, controls and barriers to entry either by governments or from monopolistic practices, exclusive contracts, etc, by firms, should be minimized.

Besides ease of entry into the product and business markets, the existence of capital or financial markets to limit, transfer or spread risks are also conducive to innovation. These markets provide the means to limit the financial loss of failure to the innovator because, he can raise capital from other investors to share the financial risk with him. Furthermore, in the event that the innovation is a great success, the inventor can sell his invention to reap the rewards of his success and exit from the business to concentrate on some other activity.

An *Ex-Poste* Market "Selection System"

An innovator must be assured of a "fair" chance of being chosen for success for his efforts. The free market is a better impartial "selection system" than one, where the selection is done by a panel of individuals or experts. Market selection is *ex-poste* in contrast to the *ex-ante* judgement of experts. The danger of depending on *ex-ante* selection lies in the inability of humans to predict the future from the trends of the past. History is full of mistaken prognoses of innovations by "experts" who fail to correctly assess the potential of a truly novel idea. For e.g., a British Parliamentary Committee commenting on Thomas Edison's light bulb said, "... good enough for our transatlantic friends ... but unworthy of the attention of practical or scientific men". Edison himself said "Fooling around with alternating current is just a waste of time. Nobody will use it, ever".[1] Today, life is impossible without alternating current.

Capital markets, venture capital funds and angel funds that seek out emergent innovations and are prepared to take higher risks, play a critical bridging role between the initial idea and eventual success in the market place. These funds select innovation *ex-poste* at different stages of their development, and are managed by risk takers and entrepreneurs who thrive on diversity and risks. It is therefore not surprising that innovations such as Yahoo, Google, etc, thrive in the Silicon Valley where the capital and product markets converge so favorably.

Sustaining Reward System

Whilst a large part of an innovator's reward may be psychological and non-material, he certainly would enjoy and deserve the material rewards that accompany his success. Such material rewards have to

---

[1] Some famous examples of flawed prognoses:

"I think there is a world market for maybe five computers".
- Thomas Watson, Chairman of IBM, 1943

"There is no reason anyone would want a computer in their home".
- Ken Olson, President, Chairman and Founder of Digital Equipment Corp., 1977

"This 'telephone' has too many shortcomings to be seriously considered as a means of communication. The device is inherently of no value to us".
- Western Union internal memo, 1876

"The wireless music box has no imaginable commercial value. Who would pay for a message sent to nobody in particular"?
- David Sarnoff's Associates in response to his urgings for investment in the radio in the 1920s

"Heavier-than-air flying machines are impossible".
- Lord Kelvin, President, Royal Society, 1895

"Fooling around with alternating current is just a waste of time. Nobody will use it, ever".
- Thomas Edison, 1889

be protected and sustained if innovation is to be encouraged. Hence, transparency of the reward system and a sound legal and institutional framework in which individuals are protected against arbitrary incursions on their property and other economic rights especially, intellectual property rights, is vital. Alan Greenspan has explained in eloquent detail why these requirements constitute a crucial pillar of a successful economy (Greenspan, 2007).

Sustaining the reward system is not confined to a respect for property rights. Overly high rates of income taxation have the effect of expropriating the innovator's return. From the innovation angle, taxation on consumption is favored over income taxation. A taxation regime that is non-transparent or changed arbitrarily also increases risks to the innovator.

SINGAPORE'S RECORD

Singapore performs well on all 4 criteria mentioned above except for, the criterion of market size. Information and knowledge flow freely throughout the economy with rare exceptions (mainly on social grounds). The education system does an excellent job of O-type innovation training, up to tertiary levels and beyond. Foreign companies and invesors are encouraged to bring in their technology, skills and people (with skills) along with their investments and they can operate in Singapore, with practically no restrictions. New companies can be set up in Singapore, with the greatest of ease and at low cost. Economic policies are chosen on sound economic rational principles based on the freely competing market model, except where there are over-riding social reasons. Free competition is assured consistently through policies and by legislation. Property rights are enforced and stability of that protection is ensured. Tax policies have increasingly favored production rather than consumption and the tax rates on income have been progressively reduced. There are no arbitrary changes in tax laws.

On the negative side, Singapore's economy *per se* does not have the size, breadth or depth of markets (both physical and financial) to sustain a high rate of V-type innovation. V-type innovation is a function of diversity which in turn is related to size and scale. This point is illustrated by Bill Gates' observation that Microsoft would put a research center only in places with a population of 1 billion or more, hence one center each for China, India and Europe.[2]

Improved education, skills and knowledge can multiply the effectiveness of O-type innovation but these measures can do little for V-type innovation. This explains why the state has chosen to intervene by offering grants in aid to companies and research centers as a means of compensating for the market weakness in support of V-type innovation. This approach is sensible but the danger of *ex-ante* planning even with the best of intentions should be noted.

The book "Good Capitalism, Bad Capitalism", analyses 4 types of capitalism: state-guided capitalism, oligarchic capitalism, big-firm capitalism, and entrepreneurial capitalism. It concluded that entrepreneurial capitalism is best for promoting and sustaining long term growth (William *et al.*, 2007). The authors envisaged that an economy with many (usually small) entrepreneurial firms provides the wherewithal to generate long term economic growth and prosperity in collaboration with the bigger firms which are more likely to be in a position to refine the innovations from the smaller firms. This is very similar to the conclusion drawn from the analysis of the innovation cycle above. The book also concluded that state-guided capitalism is not necessarily optimal for sustained high growth, particularly when the country has already attained a relatively advanced level of development. Singapore's economy is classified as a form of state-guided capitalism and by implication, its growth should be less than optimal.

Singapore proves to be an exception and enjoys high rates of growth because, its economy should not be viewed as an entity by itself but as part of a global network. Since the 1960's, Singapore has opened up its economy and welcomed MNCs and Foreign Direct Investments so as to plug itself into the global economy and in particular, the US economy. This approach was so contrary to the conventional economic wisdom of the 1960's that, many experts called it a "folly".

[2] Conversation 30 June 2005.

Singapore thus becomes a part of the global networked economy and shares the benefit of growth powered by the larger, transnational innovation cycle. The need to plug into the global innovation cycle therefore provided another reason for the open trade and investment policies pursued by Singapore in addition to the usual argument for free trade, based on David Ricardo's theorem of comparative advantage and specialization in production.

Plugging into this innovation cycle is more than just engaging in trade. It involves actively encouraging foreign companies from countries with well-developed markets to bring their technology (O-type innovation) and research activities (V-type innovation) to Singapore. By coming to Singapore, these companies bring with them their knowledge and access of markets as well as their knowledge of emergent innovations overseas. They act like "transport agents" connecting Singapore into the cycle of innovation and information exchange with their home markets in addition to their production and trading activities.

The huge importing power of the US market has given rise to the saying that "when the US economy sneezes, the rest of the world catches a cold". The current analysis shows that it is not just raw importing power that matters. It is that the US provides large, sophisticated markets for the innovation cycle to work and then the process of free trade and cross-border investments spread the innovation and production gains to other countries that freely trade with it.[3] Conversely, innovation is needed to drive and sustain economic growth and hence markets. This gives rise to the symbiotic relationship between markets and innovation. Innovation needs markets as much as markets need innovation.

Since innovation is so crucial for long economic growth and so symbiotically linked to markets, policy makers in government have to pay careful attention to how their policies affect the flow of

[3] Of course whether the US will continue to play this role is the subject of another topic. It is conceivable that some other regions or countries may take over this role of "economic engine". For the moment, however, the US continues a play a big role in this process.

information, the structure of their markets, and the regulations and institutions concerning property rights.

END NOTES

Greenspan, A (2007). *The Age of Turbulence*. Penguin Press.

William, JB, RE Litan and CJ Schramm (2007). *Good Capitalism, Bad Capitalism*. Yale University Press.

Chapter

3

Macro Objectives of the Central Provident Fund (CPF): A Review

*Chew Soon Beng and Rosalind Chew**

This chapter examines the changing roles of the CPF scheme as the Singapore economy develops, society matures and globalization intensifies. The original purpose of the scheme was to encourage saving for old age but it was extended to cover the goal of home ownership which reinforces savings. However, the CPF scheme was also used as an instrument to increase labor cost to motivate employers to better manage the use of labor in the late 1970s and early 1980s, which boosted the residential markets, and used as a cost-cutting devise to reduce labor cost in 1986, which compromised the goals of the CPF. Since the mid-1990s, as a result of globalization, the wages of low-income Singaporeans were tied to the wages of those countries with a huge labor surplus such as China and India. Consequently, the income gap has been widening in Singapore. Today, the goal of the CPF scheme is to ensure that low-income Singaporeans have sufficient savings to see them through old age, which is a challenge, as life expectancy has increased and the markets for low-wage jobs have diminished.

* The authors are indebted to Ms Loo Sock Min of the CPF Board for clarifications on many aspects of the CPF scheme. Usual disclaimers apply.

THE CENTRAL PROVIDENT FUND SCHEME, (1955–65): STATUS QUO

The Central Provident Fund (CPF) scheme was set up in 1955 to serve as the main form of social security for workers after retirement in Singapore (Lim *et al.*, 1986 gives an extensive discussion on social security schemes and the CPF). It is a compulsory saving scheme required by law of all employees. In 1995, under the CPF scheme, an employee with a monthly pay of, e.g., S$100 must, according to the law, contribute 5 percent of his pay towards his CPF account (see Table 1). At the same time, his employer was also required by law to contribute, 5 percent of the worker's pay towards the same account for the worker. Thus, every month, the employee would have CPF savings of S$10 and his take-home pay would be S$90. The cost of employing this worker therefore amounted to S$110. The cost of employing the worker is therefore affected by the employer's contribution rate. Consequently, a wage ceiling was put in place, and it was initially set at S$500. This means that, for a person earning S$600 a month, for instance, his employer would still contribute 5% of S$500 instead of 5% of S$600. The monthly wage ceiling aims to prevent labor costs from escalating beyond proportion.

CPF members could not withdraw their CPF saving until the age of 55. The CPF Board invests the CPF money in government stocks and pays the CPF member an interest of 2.5% per annum on his CPF balances, with the possibility of the interest rate rising to as high as 5% (CPF 2004). As the rate of 2.5% is assured by the CPF Board, it is considered a high rate of return for a riskless investment.

Many workers voiced their dissatisfaction with the fact that they could not drawn on their CPF saving in emergencies such as unemployment and sickness, but the CPF Board stood firm (The Straits Times, 21 April 1955). On hindsight, the CPF decision has been the correct one. Had the CPF funds been allowed to be drawn for emergencies, the CPF scheme would have been a failure as workers would withdraw their CPF saving for one reason or another. Later in the chapter, we will compare the western countries' unemployment benefit scheme with the CPF scheme.

Table 1: CPF Contribution Rates (1955–2008)

Effective Date	Rates of Contribution (%)		Ordinary Account (%)	Special Account (%)	Medisave Account (%)	Total (%)
	Employer	Employee				
1955	5.0	5.0	n.a	n.a	n.a	10.0
1968	6.5	6.5	n.a	n.a	n.a	13.0
1970	8.0	8.0	n.a	n.a	n.a	16.0
1971	10.0	10.0	n.a	n.a	n.a	20.0
1972	12.0	12.0	n.a	n.a	n.a	24.0
1973	13.0	13.0	n.a	n.a	n.a	26.0
1974	15.0	15.0	n.a	n.a	n.a	30.0
1975	15.0	15.0	n.a	n.a	n.a	30.0
1976	15.0	15.0	n.a	n.a	n.a	30.0
1977	15.5	15.5	30.0	1.0	n.a	31.0
1978	16.5	16.5	30.0	3.0	n.a	33.0
1979	20.5	16.5	30.0	7.0	n.a	37.0
1980	20.5	18.0	32.0	6.5	n.a	38.5
1981	20.5	22.0	38.5	4.0	n.a	42.5
1982	22.0	23.0	40.0	5.0	n.a	45.0
1983	23.0	23.0	40.0	6.0	n.a	46.0
1984	25.0	25.0	40.0	4.0	6.0	50.0
1985	25.0	25.0	40.0	4.0	6.0	50.0
1986	10.0	25.0	25.0	4.0	6.0	35.0
1987	10.0	25.0	29.0	0.0	6.0	35.0
1988	12.0	24.0	30.0	0.0	6.0	36.0
1989	15.0	23.0	30.0	2.0	6.0	38.0
1990	16.5	23.0	30.0	3.5	6.0	39.5
1991	17.5	22.5	30.0	4.0	6.0	40.0
1992	18.0	22.0	30.0	4.0	6.0	40.0
1993	18.5	21.5	30.0	4.0	6.0	40.0
1994	20.0	20.0	30.0	4.0	6.0	40.0
1995	20.0	20.0	30.0	4.0	6.0	40.0
1996	20.0	20.0	30.0	4.0	6.0	40.0
1997	20.0	20.0	30.0	4.0	6.0	40.0
1998	20.0	20.0	30.0	4.0	6.0	40.0
1999	10.0	20.0	24.0	0.0	6.0	30.0
2000	12.0	20.0	22.0	2.0	8.0	32.0
2001	16.0	20.0	22.0	6.0	8.0	36.0

(Continued)

Table 1: *(Continued)*

Effective Date	Rates of Contribution (%)		Ordinary Account (%)	Special Account (%)	Medisave Account (%)	Total (%)
	Employer	Employee				
2002	16.0	20.0	22.0	6.0	8.0	36.0
2003	16.0	20.0	22.0	6.0	8.0	36.0
2004	13.0	20.0	22.0	5.0	6.0	33.0
2005	13.0	20.0	22.0	5.0	6.0	33.0
2006	13.0	20.0	22.0	5.0	6.0	33.0
2007	14.5	20.0	23.0	5.0	6.5	34.5
2008	14.5	20.0	23.0	5.0	6.5	34.5

Note: n.a-not applicable. Foreign workers and their employers do not contribute to the CPF.
Source: CPF Annual Reports.

Singapore obtained self-government in 1959, joined Malaysia in 1963 and became an independent country in 1965. Being a young nation, the Singapore government had many pressing issues, such as unemployment and housing, to worry about (Goh, 1972; Seng and Lim, 1984). Consequently, the CPF system as the main form of social security scheme for old age was not altered in terms of contribution rates and structure, but the CPF interest rate was increased for the first time in 1963 from 2.5% to 5% per annum.

HOME OWNERSHIP

During the two years as Malaysia and Singapore experienced two racial riots, it was thought that political and social stability would be enhanced when citizens have a stake in the economy by way of home ownership. Hence, the massive housing programme to relocate residents from the housing slums to government-built Housing Development Board (HDB) flats was intensified immediately after independence (Lim and Associates, 1988). In 1968, to enable all employed citizens to own an HDB flat, CPF members were allowed to use their CPF balance to finance the mortgage of HDB flats (CPF 2004). Hence, since its inception in 1955, the CPF scheme has served two objectives: (1) saving for old age/disablement and (2) the political objective of promoting home ownership. The following quotation from Mr Lee Kuan Yew, the founding Prime Minister of Singapore and currently the Minister Mentor, underscores the importance of home ownership:

> "*The CPF and home ownership have ensured political stability, the foundation upon which Singapore grew and developed without interruption for more than 30 years in from Third World to First*". (Lee, 2000)

The CPF scheme therefore became more complex. CPF contributors were not allowed to withdraw their CPF saving before age 55, but there was no age limit on their use of CPF saving to buy an HDB flat. As a result, practically every married man who had a full-time job would apply to buy an HDB flat (singles initially were not allowed to buy HDB flats).

The CPF rate was indirectly tied to the price of an HDB flat. In order to provide decent HDB flats, the cost of constructing the HDB flats was high, and therefore the prices of the flats, had to be raised. This meant that the CPF contribution rate had to be high enough to cover the financing of a mortgage on an HDB flat. In 1968 the CPF contribution rates were therefore accordingly raised for employees and employers to 6.5%. At the same time, the monthly wage ceiling was raised to S$2,307.95, almost five times the $500 ceiling in 1955 (Lim *et al.*, 1986). Although this meant that labor costs were much higher, employers at that time did not complain, as the economy was facing a labor shortage.

In 1970, the government saw the need to raise the CPF contribution rate to 8% for both employers and employees; but to mitigate the increase in labor costs, the wage ceiling was reduced to S$1,875. In 1971, the government again raised the CPF contribution rates to 10% and at the same time lowered the wage ceiling to S$1,500. It should be noted that in 1972, pensionable government officers were required to make CPF contributions at a reduced rate (but this chapter focuses on employees in the private sector). In 1974, due to the extremely tight labor market, both the CPF contribution rates for employers and employees were raised to 15% and the wage ceiling increased to S$2,000.

It is obvious that the CPF scheme was biased in favor of residential investment. Indeed, many Singaporean households emptied their CPF balances to finance HDB mortgages. At the same time, the government also encouraged Singaporean households to upgrade from a small unit to a larger unit. It was thought that excessive investment in residential property was slightly inconsistent with the original objective of the CPF scheme which was purely to provide for old age living and disablement (many studies examine the housing issue and other economic issues, including Lim and Associates 1988 and Krause *et al.*, 1987).

SPLIT OF THE CPF ACCOUNT

In 1977, to address this problem, the CPF account was divided into two accounts, the Ordinary Account and Special Account. The CPF saving in the Ordinary Account could be used to finance the mortgage of a purchase of a HDB flat while the CPF saving in the Special Account was not allowed to be used. In the same year, the government also raised the CPF contribution rates to 15.5% each. Of the total 31%, 30% was allocated to the Ordinary Account and 1% the Special Account. Interestingly, in 1978, CPF members were allowed to use up to S$5,000 from the Ordinary Account for the purchase of shares. This reflected a new government policy to enable citizens to have a bigger stake in the economy by allowing more people to own other assets including shares, besides properties.

CPF AS AN ECONOMIC RESTRUCTURING TOOL

Right from the late 1960s to the mid-1970s, the Singapore economy encountered a labor shortage due to its success in attracting labor-intensive industries. Since labor costs were not high at that time, the economy attracted mainly labor-intensive industries which in turn increased the demand for low-wage labor, many of whom were foreign labor. In the late 1970s, when China was in the midst of formulating its economic reform strategy, the Singapore government became aware of the danger of being caught in a low-wage trap and saw the immediate need to restructure the manufacturing sector towards more high-skilled and capital-intensive technology. To encourage employers to shift to more high-skilled and capital-intensive methods, the government raised labor costs by increasing the CPF contribution rates to 16.5% in 1978 and raising the wage ceiling to S$3,000. At the same time, the Skills Development Fund was set up to provide subsidies to encourage employers to train their workers (for an extensive examination of this economic restructuring issue, see Lim, 1984).

HOME PROTECTION INSURANCE SCHEME USING CPF SAVING

In 1981, the home ownership plan was widened to include private properties (non-HDB flats). Hence, CPF members were allowed to use their saving in the Ordinary Account for the purchase of private properties. However, few people bought residential properties without a housing mortgage. There was this danger that a family could lose the residential property if its bread-winner dies early and the family could not continue to pay the monthly installment. Hence, in late 1981, it was legislated that the saving in the Ordinary Account could also be used to pay for the premium for the Home Protection Insurance Scheme (HPIS). HPIS guarantees the true meaning of home ownership for the family.

The rise in CPF contribution rates and the higher wage ceiling reinforced the original objective of the CPF, which is to ensure that Singaporeans have sufficient money including assets for retirement. Employed Singaporeans had never had it so good. Hence, to meet the many demands on the CPF funds, the CPF contribution rates were raised to 23% for both employer and employee in 1983. In March 1984, CPF members were allowed to use their saving in the Ordinary Account for the purchase of second properties. This new policy initiative went beyond the objective of home ownership. It aimed to encourage Singaporean families to continue to work hard, which is the inevitable outcome if they had more than one housing mortgage.

AFFORDABLE HEALTH AS THE NEW OBJECTIVE OF THE CPF SCHEME

In the late 1970s, besides worrying about China's implementation of economic reform, the Singapore government was also alerted by the fact that healthcare spending as a percentage of GDP was rising in the developed countries. Although there are many reasons contributing to the rapid rise in healthcare spending, the price for the use of healthcare facilities was distorted in the West. Accordingly, the Singapore government started to restructure the public hospitals. The inevitable outcome was to raise the price of usage of hospitals to stem unwanted and unjustified demands and usages. At the same time, the government was aware that some Singaporeans might have a problem paying for the new charges.

Hence, the CPF scheme was restructured into three accounts, the Ordinary Account, the Special Account and the newly-added Medisave Account. The CPF balance in the Medisave account could be used to meet the expenses of hospitalization. At the same time, the CPF contribution rates for employers and employees were further raised to 25% in 1984. All of the resulting additional six percentage would be channeled into the Medisave Account. As the wage ceiling of the CPF scheme was also raised to S$5,000 in 1984 and to S$6,000 in 1985, labor costs in Singapore were considered high.

The CPF balance in the Medisave Account was originally intended to cover the cost of use of public hospitals, but in 1985 the Medisave Scheme was extended to include use of private hospitals. The Medisave Account is actually meant for the family, as the greater part of the expenses of hospitalization for a male employee, his wife and his children under the age of 18 years would be paid by his employer. However, in the case of a female employee, coverage for her children and her spouse are not included in her fringe benefits scheme. Hence the money in the Medisave Account would be expedient in the event of the hospitalization of a spouse, child or a parent. The Medisave

Account has a ceiling of S$5,000. Once it is reached, the monthly share of Medisave Account will be channeled to the Ordinary Account. Nevertheless, the creation of the Medisave Account added one more objective to the CPF scheme, which is to ensure that healthcare is affordable and sustainable (see Tan and Chew 1997 for a discussion on healthcare issues).

CPF AS A PRINCIPAL TOOL FOR THE REDUCTION OF LABOR COSTS

The Singapore economy grew strongly in early 1985, but exports began to fall later that year as the global economy went into a recession. This was exacerbated by the strong Singapore dollar and the high labor costs (for causes of recession at that time, see Lim and Associates, 1988). This shows that, for Singapore, quarterly economic figures are important for decision-making. With the fall in exports, unemployment surged. As Singapore's social safety net, which is provided by the CPF scheme is employment-based, the government had to decide whether to lower the wage costs immediately, or devalue Singapore dollar, or institute a western-style social welfare system. The course decided upon was a reduction of the employer's CPF contribution rate from 25% to 10%, with the entire 15% reduction to be taken from the Ordinary Account. Many Singaporeans were caught off guard as they had used every dollar in their Ordinary Account for their housing mortgages and took the maximum amount of loan permitted to buy properties. Consequently, some of them could not meet their monthly mortgage payments. However, the government immediately assured the public that the loan period could be extended by 5 more years if necessary. Nevertheless, the recession was worsened by the fact that there were many foreclosures in the property market due to the change in CPF ruling on the employer's contribution rate. In 1987, the government realized the adverse impact and therefore redirected 4 of the percentage points, which were meant for the Special Account, into the Ordinary Account, thus restoring the percentage for the Ordinary Account from 25% to 29% (see Table 1).

Although the employer's CPF contribution rate was reduced by 15%, the CPF Board expanded the usage of the CPF scheme. In 1985, CPF members could use their saving in the Ordinary Account to buy more than one residential property. In 1986, CPF members were allowed to use their CPF saving in the Ordinary Account to purchase non-residential properties, gold, shares and unit trusts. The rationale is obvious. Although the rate of return on CPF balances is considered high as it is almost guaranteed, some CPF members wanted a higher rate of return on their CPF saving. Hence the expanded usage of the CPF saving was mandated. However, the CPF Board kept reminding Singaporeans that investment in property, stocks, shares and gold carry both the opportunity for capital gains and the risk of capital loss (CPF, 2004).

The fact that the CPF scheme was the principal tool to lower wage costs, leading to the drastic decrease in the employer CPF contribution rate, had compromised the original goal of the CPF which was to ensure that Singaporeans had sufficient assets for old age (Lim and Associates, 1988).

CPF SAVING AND THE MINIMUM SUM SCHEME

Since the early 1980s, the government became aware that some of the Singaporeans were not able to effectively manage their CPF saving when they withdrew it upon reaching the age of 55. Consequently, for some of them, the lifetime saving did not last long enough. This caused hardship at the family level. Meanwhile, life expectancy had increased. At the same time, the government was planning to increase the retirement age from 55 to 60. Hence, to ensure that CPF members would have some money at hand to cope with the longer life expectancy, it was legislated in 1987 that, CPF members must set aside a minimum sum of S$30,000 in their CPF at the age of 55. There are three options for CPF members to manage this S$30,000: (1) to buy a life annuity from a participating insurance company with which they would be paid a monthly income from age 62 until death, (2) to deposit the money with a participating bank which would yield an interest, and the bank would pay the members a monthly income until the minimum sum is exhausted, (3) to continue to let the CPF manage the CPF balances with a guaranteed return of 4%. The CPF again would pay the member a monthly income until the minimum sum is exhausted. Singaporeans do not like the idea of the annuity as they feel that they would be short-changed upon early death. Hence, most people took the CPF option.

The government now encourages CPF members who are about to receive their retirement payments at the age of 62 to defer withdrawal to the age of 65. If they agree to defer withdrawal of the monthly payments to the age of 65, they would get S$600 per year under the Voluntary Deferment Bonus (VDB). VDB is paid by the government and not the CPF Board. It is estimated that more than 10,000 CPF members will reach 63 or 64 by 2008 and will be entitled to qualify for the VDB. Those who have withdrawn their monthly payments at the age of 62 or 63 are allowed to return the money to their own retirement accounts and enjoy the VDB.

CONTROVERSY OVER THE MINIMUM SUM SCHEME

The minimum sum is currently raised to S$99,600. As most people opted for the CPF saving option, the government feels that many people may outlive their savings. Consequently, it has been proposed that the annuity be made compulsory for CPF members but on a smaller scale. While the details have not been finalized, the main proposal is that for those who are not yet 50 years of age, when they reach the age of 55, they would need to use about S$9,000 to buy an annuity scheme, for which they would be paid a monthly sum of S$250 starting from the age of 85 until death. The debate focuses on the starting age for receiving the monthly sum and whether the annuity can be combined with an element of saving in case the person insured dies soon after the policy takes effect.

The National Longevity Insurance Committee has proposed to the government that a compulsory annuity scheme that will provide elderly Singaporeans with a regular income for as long as they live be introduced in 2013 (Straits Times, 13 February 2008). The salient features are as follows: at age 55, the minimum sum will be kept under the Retirement Account which is still managed by the CPF Board. One part will pay for the CPF Life premium. This portion is pooled together with the premiums of other CPF Life members. The other part remains in the Retirement Account and earns interest from the CPF Board. For those whose minimum sum exceeds S$40,000, they will start to receive an income from the sum in the Retirement Account from the age of 65 to 80 (actually, the period is flexible). At the age of 80, CPF members will start to receive an income from CPF Life for life. Should a CPF member die earlier, there will be a refund, the amount of which will be equal to the CPF Life premium minus the CPF payouts he had received. It goes without saying that the payout is greater if there is no refund. For those whose minimum sum is less than S$40,000, the government has to help to top up the minimum sum.

Workers who qualify for the Workfare programme (which will be discussed later) are not likely to have much CPF money. In all probability, their CPF balances will be less than S$40,000 when they reach the age of 55. We propose that the government start helping these workers from as early as when they are in their mid-30s, by matching their CPF contributions proportionally by a factor of, say, 0.5–2 each year, and channeling this top-up amount into the Special Account to help them build up their minimum sum. E.g., if the top-up matching factor is 0.5, if a worker contributes S$500 to his CPF account in a year, the government will match his contribution by topping up this worker's Special Account by S$250. If the top-up matching factor is 2, then the government will top up his Special Account by S$1,000. As these top-up matching amounts from the government will only be awarded if the worker is in employment and as they are channeled into the worker's minimum sum, such a policy will motivate workers to remain in employment. Hopefully, with the implementation of such a top-up, fewer workers will not have insufficient sum at the age of 55.

RESTORATION OF THE EMPLOYER CPF CONTRIBUTION RATE SINCE 1988

The recovery from the 1985 recession was, fortunately, almost immediate. Consequently, the employer's CPF contribution rate was raised to 12% in 1988; but in order to give Singaporeans more disposable income, the employee's CPF contribution rate was lowered from 25% to 24%. Hence, there was 30% for the Ordinary Account, 0% for the Special Account and 6% for the Medisave Account. After that year, the Singapore economy consolidated. By 1990, the employer and employee rates had been revised to 16.5% and 23% respectively. The rate for the Special Account was raised to 3.5%.

USAGE OF THE CPF EXTENDED TO TERTIARY EDUCATION

In 1989, for the first time CPF members were allowed to draw their CPF savings to finance tertiary education in Singapore for themselves or their children. But the money used for tertiary education, whether for members themselves or their children, have to be repaid with interest within 10 years.

LIFE AND MEDICAL INSURANCE INTRODUCED INTO THE CPF SCHEME

The CPF is a saving scheme, but an insurance element is introduced into the system when CPF members are able to use their CPF saving to insure themselves and therefore provide their dependants with financial protection should death or permanent disability occur. This was initiated in 1989, when CPF members were permitted to use their CPF saving to buy a term-life insurance covering members against death or permanent disability. Furthermore, many CPF members even bought personal life insurance with cash, especially when they purchased private properties.

The money in the Medisave Account and for that matter in the CPF scheme is inadequate should a member suffer from long-term illness. Hence, in 1990, CPF members were permitted to use their CPF money to pay for the premium for MediShield, which is a medical insurance scheme to help members pay for expenses incurred in long term and serious illnesses. This scheme was also extended to the self-employed in 1992 (again, the CPF scheme is basically meant for employees in the private sector).

INCREASING THE STAKE IN THE COUNTRY

As home ownership had been successfully achieved by the 1980s, the government wanted to help Singaporeans increase their stake in the country. Hence, in 1993, every Singaporean was given a chance to buy Singapore Telecom shares at a discounted rate using their CPF money, (Singapore Telecom is a government-linked corporation). For those who did not have a CPF account or insufficient money in their CPF account, they could open an account with a minimum deposit of S$50 or their children or parents could deposit either cash or transfer their CPF money to their CPF account for them to purchase the shares.

In 2001, adult Singaporeans who had contributed at least S$50 to their CPF account during that year would receive between 200 and 1,700 New Singapore Shares (NSS) if they were not employed. This is social welfare or unemployment benefit. But the money received went straight into the CPF account to be used either for old age, payments for housing mortgage or payments for hospitalization. The same practice was repeated in 2003, when all Singaporeans who had deposited at least S$50 into their CPF account in the previous year, received their Economic Restructuring Shares.

DISTRIBUTION OF NATIONAL WEALTH VIA THE CPF TOP-UP SCHEME

The government encourages all Singaporeans to have a CPF account. As one form of encouragement, in 1993 the government offered to transfer S$200 to the CPF account of any Singaporean whose CPF balance is in excess of S$500. This is known as the CPF Top-Up Scheme. Many Singaporeans transferred their CPF money to the CPF accounts of their parents and children to take advantage of this scheme.

The CPF Top-Up exercise was repeated again in 1995. The government used the Top-up scheme to distribute national wealth by paying

S$200 to every adult Singaporean's Ordinary Account. In the same year, the government also topped up the Medisave Accounts of Singaporeans aged 61 and above with amounts ranging from S$100 to S$350 on the condition that they have contributed S$50 into their Medisave Account during a 6-month period. Again, CPF members were encouraged to transfer their CPF money to the Medisave Accounts of their parents to take advantage of the Medisave Top-Up Scheme. Another Medisave Top-up exercise was carried out in 1997 by the government. Under that exercise, S$100 was transferred to the CPF accounts of all Singaporeans below the age of 60 and S$200 to those above 60. A total S$229 million was paid out under that exercise. In the year 2000, another CPF top-up exercise by the government saw the CPF Ordinary Account of Singaporeans increasing by S$250. In 2007, the government gave one extra percentage in interest to all CPF saving up to a maximum of S$60,000. This extra payment is meant to benefit low-income Singaporeans.

CHANGING EMPHASIS FROM INVESTMENT TO HEALTHCARE

In 1992, the employer and employee contribution rate was changed to 18% and 22% respectively. By then, the government was more concerned about affordable health as home ownership has been achieved with great success. The percentage contribution for the Ordinary Account and the Medisave Account was 30% and 6% respectively for those aged 35 and below. But for those aged between 35 to 55 years, the percentage contribution for the Ordinary Account and the Medisave Account was 29% and 7% account. As expected, the CPF structure is not targeted at those older than 55 years, and therefore it is not surprising that the employer's contribution rate for this group of employees is very low, 3% or less, with most of the contribution going into the Medisave Account.

In 1994, the employer's and employee's contribution rate was 20% each. For those aged 35 years and below, the percentage contribution for the Ordinary Account was 30%, 4% for the Special Account and 6% for the Medisave account. For those aged 35 to 45, the respective contribution was 29%, 4% and 7%. For those aged 45 to 55, the respective contribution was 28%, 4% and 8%. These changes show the deliberate policy shift away from Ordinary Account to Medisave Account. This is further underlined by the fact that a contribution ceiling for the Medisave Account of S$33,500 is in place, and that any amount in excess of S$33,500 in the Medisave Account would be channeled into the Special Account instead of the Ordinary Account. The monthly wage ceiling was left unchanged at S$6,000.

INCREASING THE RATE OF RETURN ON CPF SAVING

The CPF savings do earn an interest. It is 2.5% on the savings in the Ordinary Account and 4% on the other two accounts. Considering that it is practically riskless, the rate of return is very high. However, this was not much an issue in the 1970s because most people use the money for property investment, the price of which has risen many times, some CPF members wanted a higher rate of return for the compulsory savings. Hence, in 1997, the government set up the CPF Investment Scheme to allow members to enjoy a wider range of investment options.

THE EAST ASIAN CURRENCY CRISIS AND THE SUCCEEDING YEARS

The Singapore economy was very much affected by the currency crisis in 1997 (Lim, 2000). The Singapore dollar depreciated against the US dollar by 19% but the stock market and property index went down by as much as 50%. Singaporeans were as expected, very badly hurt as Singapore has now become a nation of property owners and share owners. But the falling value of the Singapore dollar did help the country to export more to the markets in the developed countries and the rising value of the Singapore dollar relative to regional currencies gave Singaporeans more purchasing power to import things from ASEAN countries. However, the financial sector was badly affected and the construction sector totally collapsed, creating negative multiple effects. The unemployment rate surged.

Due to our inability to use the flexible wage system to lower the wage cost (Chew *et al.*, 2005), the employer's CPF contribution rate was lowered to 10% in 1999 (see Table 1). This time the government was more prepared, and the 10 percentage points came from six points from the Ordinary Account and 4 points from the Special Account. The 4 percentage points for the Medisave Account were left untouched.

The economy rebounded in 1999 and accordingly, the employer's contribution rate was raised to 12% in 2000 and 16% in 2001. For the Singapore economy, that was a period of painful transition, with the private sector undergoing wage reform and some of the big government-linked corporations conducting labor rationalization exercises (Chew *et al.*, 2003). Consequently, GDP growth was low during 2001 to 2003. In fact, Singapore's GDP growth was worse than that of its ASEAN neighbors in 2001 because, among other factors, domestic sentiment was poor (Chew, 2006). Consequently, unemployment rate in Singapore was very high. When Singapore, along with Hong Kong, China and Taiwan, was affected by SARS in 2003 and the services sector was badly hurt, causing the unemployment surge to a new high, the government had no choice but to trim labor costs again by lowering the employer's CPF contribution rate to 13% and the monthly wage ceiling was reduced to S$5,500 in 2004. Again, the flexible wage system could not bail us out (Chew *et al.*, 2005).

WORRY OVER OLDER WORKER'S EMPLOYMENT

The government is rightly very preoccupied with the ageing of the population on one hand and competitiveness on the other. Realizing that older workers may not be as competitive as younger workers and foreign workers, the government reduced the employer's CPF contribution rate for workers older than 50 years in 2005. As a result, while the employer's contribution rate for workers below the age of 50 was 13%, the employer's contribution rate for workers aged 50 to 55 was reduced from 11% in 2005 to 9% in 2006. The employer's contribution rate is 6% for workers older than 55 years and 3.5% for those older than 60 years (CPF Annual Report, 2006). (The employee's contribution rate, too, was reduced to 19% in 2005 and again to 18% in 2006).

Hence, for workers below the age of 50, the employer's and employee's CPF contribution rate was 13% and 20%, respectively. There are concerns that Singaporeans might have a liquidity problem after retirement. Hence, in 2006, the respective contribution for the Ordinary Account, Special Account and Medisave Account for those aged 35 and below was set at 22%, 5% and 6%, for those aged 35 to 45, the respective contribution rate was 20%, 6% and 7%, for those aged 45 to 50, the respective contribution rate was 18%, 7% and 8% and for those aged between 50 to 55, the respective contribution rate was 18%, 7% and 8%. Clearly, there has been a deliberate policy to de-emphasize the investment objective.

HIGHER CONTRIBUTION RATES FOR OLD AGE AND HEALTHCARE

2006 was a good year for Singapore. Accordingly, in 2007, the employer's contribution rate was raised to 14.5% for workers below 50 years of age and 10.5% for workers between 50 to 55 years of age (no change in employee's contribution rate). Again, the government wants more savings to be channeled into the Special and Medisave Accounts. Hence, for workers younger than 35 years of age, the respective CPF contribution for the Ordinary, the Special Account and the Medisave Account was 23%, 5% and 7%, while for workers between 35 to 45 years of age, the respective CPF contribution was 21%, 6% and 8%, for workers aged 45 to 50, the respective CPF contribution was 19%, 7% and 9% and, for workers aged 50 to 55, the CPF contribution was 13%, 7% and 9%.

FINE-TUNING TO HELP YOUNG LOW-INCOME SINGAPOEANS IN COMPETITION WITH FOREIGNERS

There is a concern that young low-income Singaporeans may find it difficult to get a job because of competition from foreign workers.

Hence the CPF contribution rate is tweaked to counter this problem. Thus, while the employer's CPF contribution rate is 14.5% for workers aged between 35 to 45 years whose monthly wage is S$1,500 or more, it is 11.7% for those in this age group whose monthly wage is S$1,000, and 9.7% if the monthly wage is S$800 or below. The reasoning is acceptable. Lower employer CPF contribution may encourage employers to employ them instead of employing foreigners.

One might argue that these low-income Singaporeans who are lowly educated need their CPF saving much more than high-income Singaporeans. Hence, to counter the lower employer's CPF contribution rates, the government has implemented the Workfare Income Supplement Scheme to help these low-income Singaporeans. Provided they work at least 6 months, those who earn, for instance, S$800 a month will get a monthly payment of S$100 for a year, S$29 of which will be in cash and the remaining S$71 would be deposited into the worker's CPF account. It is estimated that about 287,000 workers would receive S$146 million in Workfare Income Supplements on 1 January 2008 (of course, it goes without saying that this amount comes from the government coffers and not from the CPF board).

CPF SCHEME NOT ATTRACTIVE FOR HIGH INCOME SINGAPOREANS

The monthly wage ceiling, which had risen to S$6,000 in 2003, was reduced to S$5,000 in 2005 and again to S$4,500 in 2006. Hence, high-income Singaporeans, especially those who earn more than S$6,000 a month, no long find the CPF scheme attractive. Singapore employers have to increase the monthly pay to be commensurate with their counterparts in Hong Kong and the West if firms want them to work in Singapore.

It is obvious that with globalization, the wages of low-income Singaporeans would not rise much as they have to compete with workers from Malaysia, China and India. On the other hand, high-income Singaporeans are very mobile. Many developed countries such as USA, UK, Australia, etc., also have similar schemes where employers contribute about 10–15% of the salary of their employees into their retirement schemes. The only difference is that in these countries, there is no monthly wage ceiling. Hence, the total salary package of top professionals in Singaporeans has to be much higher because of the low wage ceiling (of course, one must not fail to mention that personal income tax is much lower in Singapore than that in developed countries). This partially explains the rising wage gap in Singapore.

CPF AS A SUSTAINABLE SOCIAL SAFETY NET

The CPF scheme has now evolved into a sustainable social safety net for low-income Singaporeans. It forces low-income Singaporeans to save for old age and motivates them to work as long as they physically can. The average monthly wage in Singapore is quite low. In 2006, more than 65% of Singaporeans earned less than S$3,000 a month and about 82% of Singaporeans had a monthly wage below S$5,000 (CPF Annual Report 2006). Hence, with the wage ceiling of S$4,500, it can be argued that the CPF scheme is more for low-income Singaporeans. On the other hand, with the low contribution from the employers and the low wage ceiling, high-income Singaporeans might migrate to the developed countries. Some people even argue that the pay in Malaysia is not as low as it appears because in Malaysia, employers pay 15% and there is no wage ceiling. The high employee CPF contribution in Singapore is viewed as negative for the high-income mobile Singaporeans because it is not matched by the employers.

MACRO IMPACT OF THE CPF SCHEME

The CPF scheme has the following impacts on the individual worker and the country:

1. **Impact on Work and Skill Level**
   The CPF scheme is a compulsory saving scheme. The level of saving depends on the worker's wages, which in turn depend on his

continued active participation in the labor market. If he changes his place of employment, the CPF scheme would continue with the new employer, as the CPF scheme is a national saving scheme.

The CPF scheme encourages workers to work hard (Lim, CY and Associates 1988). It also provides an incentive for workers to take training seriously as a worker's pay depends on his skills, which he can acquire or upgrade through training. If a worker is suddenly retrenched in Singapore, he is not allowed to withdraw his CPF balances to maintain his lifestyle. He would be told to get another job.

The CPF scheme is different from the unemployment benefits scheme that can be found in some developed countries. The unemployment benefits scheme is subject to inherent disadvantages. Firstly, it inevitably increases the reservation wage rate, which will erode a country's competitiveness. Secondly, the unemployment scheme is likely to run into deficit, which must be financed by raising tax revenue. This implies that income tax rates would be high, which will discourage people from working for more income. The CPF scheme, on the other hand, is a fully funded scheme that encourages workers to give their best in the labor market and does not need the government to subsidize it.

2. **Impact on Government Budget Policy**

The basic objective of the CPF scheme is to ensure that Singaporeans save for housing, medical expenses and old age. Singaporeans are able to save as long as they work. Jobs are plentiful in Singapore because Singapore's system of industrial relations encourages employment (Krause *et al.*, 1987). Thus, as a result of the CPF scheme, home ownership in Singapore is one of the highest among the countries in the world.

Because of the CPF scheme, the government spending on welfare in terms of housing, retirement and healthcare is minimal in Singapore. Due to high GDP growth and low welfare spending, the government has resources and is able to implement a strong exchange rate policy to reduce imported prices if necessary which in turn will stablize cost of living and protect low-income Singaporeans.

3. The CPF is an excellent instrument for implementing transfer payments, subsidies, unemployment benefits, workfare, education, etc. It can also encourage family closeness as CPF members can top up the CPF accounts of their relatives to take advantage of various government incentive schemes, It also encourages self-employed and part-time workers to enter into the fold of the CPF family. In other words, to qualify for the various share and top-up schemes, the self-employed and the odd-job workers have to declare their earnings to the CPF even though they work in the informal sector. Of course, the best part of using the CPF route for transfer payments to the needy families is that the money is channeled to the specific purposes. The money from the government distributed via the CPF route therefore cannot be diverted for purposes for which it is not intended, such as tours.
4. The CPF Board as part of the government policy uses approximately 90% of the CPF money to buy government stocks while 10% is deposited with the Monetary Authority of Singapore for operational purposes (CPF Annual Report, 2006). In return, the government promises a fixed rate of return which is why the interest rate on CPF balances has been fixed and is rather high compared to the rate of return for similar investments without risk. In other words, the government takes the risk of investment and not the CPF Board. When the government is able to raise the return from using the CPF balances or the country has enjoyed good growth rates, the government can reward CPF members in terms of CPF top-ups. This has been a good economic model to bond the people and the government.
5. Employers are expected to pay both the employer's and employee's contribution for each employee to the CPF Board monthly. If employers fail to pay the CPF contributions on time, they will be subject to some form of penalty. Many countries such as China are interested to learn about the CPF scheme. Indeed, in China, the CPF scheme has been applied to some big cities but only for the purpose of housing. A typical question from the Chinese officials is how to lower the default rate of employers and to get them to pay the CPF contribution on time, and what to

do if they fail to pay. There is actually very little that the authorities can do. If the authorities penalize the employers who fail to contribute the CPF payments stringently, they may not be able to survive, and this will hurt the workers most. In Singapore, the best policeman is not the CPF Board but the tight labor market. If the economy is doing very well, any employer who fails to pay the CPF contribution on time will lose the best workers as workers will start looking for a job elsewhere. The default rate among employers for not paying CPF contribution rate on time for two consecutive months was 0.61% in 2003 which was the worse growth year and fluctuated around 0.55% in 2006 which was a good year. In July 2007, the default rate was 0.48%.

THE CPF BOARD AND THE GOVERNMENT

The CPF Fund has been well managed. In many countries, pension funds are not well accounted for. Singapore owes its success significantly to the CPF scheme. It is worth reiterating that the CPF Board is self-financing. In some countries, the government has a budget to run a board such as the CPF Board. The CPF Board, like the Singapore government has an annual surplus (CPF Annual Report, 2006).

However, the importance of the CPF scheme diminishes because of the low employer's contribution rate and the low wage ceiling. But it is still an important scheme for low-income Singaporeans as well as for high-income Singaporeans because as employees they have to contribute 20% of their pay into the CPF account monthly.

Due to its comprehensive income data base, many ministries have been asking the CPF Board for data so that government policies can be better formulated. The CPF Board also provides agency services to the government and other organizations. For instance, it is the collecting agency for the Foreign Worker Levy and the Skills Development Levy. The CPF Board also conducts the annual Occupational Wages Survey for the Ministry of Manpower.

Recently, there has been talk about helping low-income Singaporeans through subsidies as their wages do not increase much and prices have been going up. Globalization has caused the income gap to widen at an increasing rate. We are also entering into a period of inflation. The use of bio-fuel will increase food prices. Oil prices will remain high. The markets for low pay jobs diminish. We need more resources to provide a social safety net on an even broader basis. Hence, it is imperative that only deserving Singaporeans receive government subsidies in hospitals, nursing homes, growth package, schools and universities, HDB flats for sale and rental. We can establish a single but comprehensive means testing index for all Singaporeans or for the bottom 30% of the Singaporeans.

Hence, one more function that the CPF Board is well placed to help in is, to compile a means-testing index. For instance, some people may live in HDB flats and have low reported income, but may be collecting rents from their private property. Some people who live in HDB also own properties abroad, while there are retirees living in private property who have no income. The CPF board will be in the best position to coordinate with other government agencies to compile this comprehensive index.

REVIEW AND REFLECTIONS OF THE CPF SCHEME

One ponders over the primary objective of the CPF scheme as the CPF scheme now has been used for so many purposes such as old age security, home ownership, affordable healthcare, moderating the cost of labor, and implementing the social welfare scheme. But all these are necessary for a country to manage in this open and increasingly competitive world economic environment. If we do not have the schemes for housing and healthcare and old age security, the government will have to bail people out when they are in need, and the consequence is higher government expenditures and ever-increasing budget deficits as we have seen in many countries, especially the developed countries.

However, for Singapore, these above-mentioned objectives are at times conflicting. For instance, when we lower the CPF contribution rate we compromise the objective of home ownership. But the worst problem is that when we reduce the employer's contribution rate during a recession as we did in 1986, 1999 and 2004, we also worsen the property markets. This has been the major limitation of the CPF scheme as a macro-economic instrument.

On the other hand, the CPF scheme is the most effective way to reduce labor costs. Since 1988, Singapore tried to promote the flexible wage system so that labor costs can be reduced immediately should there be a need to do so. However, it has not been very successful. Hence we had to lower the employer's CPF contribution rate in 1999 and 2004.

In fact we know that the CPF scheme is not invented by Singapore. It was a legacy from being a colony of Britain. Indeed, all British Commonwealth countries inherited the CPF scheme. Interestingly, many Commonwealth countries come to Singapore to learn why the CPF scheme has been successful in Singapore but not in their own countries.

We would like to propose, for countries which are considering implementing or revamping their CPF scheme, the following suggestions:

1. The employee's contribution to the CPF fund be devoted solely to the Housing Account (which is solely for the purpose of housing). One may argue that the contribution from only employees may not be sufficient to pay for the mortgage on a house. This is a valid argument. However, the ability to buy properties also determines the prices of properties. If we ban car loans, car prices will fall. The property prices would not be too high if only CPF contributions from employees are allowed to be used in property investment in the first place.
2. The employer's contribution to the CPF fund be allocated to three accounts: Investment Account, Retirement Account and Healthcare Account. The CPF saving in the Investment Account can be used for shares, gold, higher education, and even authorized training. All investment expenditures using the balance from the Investment Account must not require a commitment to future income (a housing mortgage commits a CPF member for payments for a period of 20 years and hence an expenditure of this nature should not be allowed for the Investment Account).

This proposal cuts the link between employer's CPF contributions and the property markets. As an economic instrument, we only need to adjust the employer's contribution rate and not the employee's contribution rate. Hence, during good times, if we have to increase labor costs, the government can raise the employer's contribution rate without giving an unwanted boost to the property market. On the other hand, during bad times, if the government cannot rely on a flexible wage system, it can lower the employer's contribution rate without affecting the property market.

CONCLUSION

This chapter examines the changing roles of the CPF scheme as the Singapore economy develops, society matures and globalization intensifies. The original aim of the CPF was to ensure that Singaporeans had sufficient saving for old age. However, the CPF scheme was extended to achieve home ownership in the mid-1960s. In the late 1970s, the CPF scheme was also used as a macro-economic instrument to restructure the manufacturing sector from labor-intensive to capital- and skills-intensive industries by increasing the contribution rate by the employers to 25% by 1984. In the same year, the CPF also was used to ensure that healthcare was affordable. The increase in CPF contribution rate reinforced the goals of savings for old age, home ownership and affordable healthcare. However, during the 1985 recession, the contribution rate of the CPF by employers was reduced by 15% as the main element of the cost-cutting measures. This compromised the goal of home ownership. Fortunately, the recession was short-lived and the CPF contribution rate was restored to 20% by 1994. However, both the 1997 currency crisis and the 2003 SARS episode had seen the employers' CPF contribution rate adjusted downwards.

During the post-9/11 period, the Singapore economy went through a painful transition with wage reform in the private sector and labor rationalization exercises in some big government-linked corporations. Fortunately, the Singapore economy had basically recovered by 2005. However, as a result of globalization, the wages of low-income Singaporeans are now tied to the wages of those countries with a huge labor surplus such as China and India. The employer's CPF contribution rate has to be kept low to ensure that low-income Singaporeans remain employable. The monthly wage ceiling to cap the employer's contribution has been lowered to $4,500 to contain labor costs. This means that employers would have to increase the salary of high-income Singaporeans in order to attract competent staff. Consequently, the income gap has been widening in Singapore.

Today, the goal of the CPF scheme is to ensure that low-income Singaporeans have sufficient compulsory saving to see them through old age, which is a challenge as life expectancy has increased and the markets for low wage jobs have diminished.

Finally, the chapter proposes that the CPF scheme can be a better macro-economic instrument if we can remove the link between the employer's contribution and the property market.

END NOTES

Central Provident Board (2004), Saving For Our Retirement: 50 Years of CPF, SNP International, Singapore.

Chew, S, L Rosalind and SB Chew (2003). Employment relations in Singapore: From flexible wage system to flexible employment system. *Employment Relations Record (Australia)*, 3(1), pp. 53–63.

Chew, SL, Rosalind and SB Chew (2005). Wage issues and human resources in Singapore. *Journal of Comparative Asian Development*, 4(1), pp. 77–103.

Chew, SB (2006). Resilience of the Singapore Economy and the Adequacy of the Social Security System. In *Singapore: Perspectives 2006*, Lai Ah Eng (ed.), Institute of Policy Studies, pp. 9–30.

Chew, SB, L Mike and KH Tan (1998). *Values and Lifestyles of Young Singaporeans*. Singapore: Prentice Hall.

Goh, KS (1972). *The Economics of Modernization and Other Essays.* Singapore: Asia Pacific Press.

Krause, L, AT Koh and Y Lee (Tsao) (1987). *The Singapore Economy Reconsidered.* Singapore: Institute of Southeast Asian Studies.

Lee, KY (2000). *From Third World to First: The Singapore Story: From 1965–2000*, HarperCollins.

Lee, TY and L Low (1990). *Local Entrepreneurship in Singapore.* Singapore: Institute of Policy Studies.

Lim, CY (1984). *Economic Restructuring in Singapore*. Singapore: Federal Publications.

Lim, CY *et al.* (1986). Report of the Central Provident Fund Study Group. *Singapore Economic Review*, Special Issue, 31(1).

Lim, CY and Associates (1988). *Policy Options for the Singapore Economy*. Singapore: McGraw Hill.

Lim, CY (2000). From recession to recovery in East Asia: A non-IMF and non-World bank explanation. *Accounting and Business Review*, 7(2), pp. 145–161.

Straits Times (2008). Annuity scheme could start in 2013, 4 February 2008, Singapore.

Tan, TM and SB Chew (1997). *Affordable Healthcare*. Singapore: Prentice Hall

Seng, YP and CY Lim (eds.) (1984). *Singapore: Twenty-Five Years of Development*. Singapore: Nan Yang Xing Zhou Lianhe Zaobao.

Chapter

4

Monetary Policy in Singapore: A BBC Approach[1]

Peter Wilson

"We have only one monetary policy, which is the exchange rate. Because we have completely open financial markets without foreign-exchange controls or capital controls, we do not even control interest rates. Our only control is managing the exchange rate and that is basically to prevent the Singapore dollar from rising too fast". (*Richard Hu Hsu Tau, Chairman of the Monetary Authority of Singapore, February 1995*)

INTRODUCTION

One of the challenging things about teaching economics in Singapore is that the uniqueness of its economy precludes the direct application of some of the standard principles of economics as prescribed, e.g., in the A-level syllabus. Monetary policy, as we shall see, is no exception.

[1] I would like to thank the participants of the NTU-Ministry of Education 2008 Seminar on Economics and Public Policy and the Staff at the Economic Policy Department, Monetary Authority of Singapore. The views expressed in this chapter are, however, solely those of the author and should not be attributed to the Monetary Authority of Singapore.

Yet Singapore cannot be ignored because it has been extremely successful when judged against the standard criteria of economic development. It has enjoyed sustained rapid economic growth since the mid-1960s, transformed itself from an entrepot trading center to a modern high value-added manufacturer and producer of high income business and financial services, and has raised the standard of living for the vast majority of its citizens to a "first-world" level (Peebles and Wilson, 2002).

In this chapter we examine Singapore's highly unusual, but very successful, monetary policy since 1981 (Monetary Authority of Singapore, 2007; Parrado, 2004; Khor *et al.*, 2007). We begin with an overview of the objectives of monetary policy, followed by a closer look at how monetary policy in Singapore is actually formulated, communicated to the general public, and implemented. We then contrast Singapore's unorthodox approach with the more "traditional" textbook approach adopted in other countries. Finally, we delve deeper into the reasons why Singapore has chosen a non-traditional approach to monetary policy and make an assessment of how successful it has been, taking into account that monetary policy does not work alone.

SINGAPORE'S EXCHANGE RATE-CENTERED MONETARY POLICY

Objectives of Monetary Policy

If you check the website of most central banks in the world you will find a similar mission statement with respect to monetary policy, namely to preserve the purchasing power of the local currency in world markets. In Singapore this means protecting the value of private savings, compulsory retirement savings with the Central Provident Fund (CPF), and Singapore's official holdings of foreign exchange reserves. During the Asian financial crisis of 1997–98 the Indonesian currency, the rupiah, fell by over 100 percent against the US dollar and other currencies and so, therefore, did the value of Indonesian assets. Would you be happy with your central bank if you were an Indonesian citizen?

Since 1981, Singapore's monetary policy has been centered on the management of the exchange rate with the primary objective of ensuring price stability as an anchor for macroeconomic stability and confidence and a sound basis for sustained economic growth. Low and stable price inflation is desirable for three main reasons. First, to provide a stable environment for domestic production and consumption. In Zimbabwe, the annual rate of inflation exceeded 100,000 percent in 2008 and a carton of orange juice cost more than 500,000 Zimbabwe dollars making it almost impossible to predict prices and creating an environment of uncertainty in which business quotes were valid only for a few days at a time and people were reluctant to hold cash for very long. Of course this is an extreme case of hyperinflation and some amount of price inflation may be desirable, but in general the lower, more stable the inflation rate, the better.

Secondly, given that much of Singapore's GDP growth comes from exports to the rest of the world, produced by multinational corporations (MNCs) based in the Republic, price stability is desirable to attract these firms and keep them operating in Singapore. Rising prices are often associated with rising wages and other costs and this might persuade MNCs to look for other locations where costs are not increasing as fast. Finally, low and stable inflation signals to the rest of the world that Singapore is a stable economy with sound macroeconomic policy and an economically safe place in which to do business, and enhances its status as an international financial center.

The BBC Exchange Rate System

Monetary policy in Singapore is essentially exchange rate policy and can be summarized in the acronym "BBC" or "basket", "band" and "crawl". The basket feature refers to the fact that the exchange rate is managed against an unpublished trade-weighted basket or index of currencies of Singapore's major trading partners and competitors. The weights in the basket are updated periodically and the basket acts as a more stable reference point for monitoring movements in the Singapore dollar than if a single currency, such as the US dollar, was used. Thus if there is a sharp fall in the US dollar, as in the first quarter of 2008, the Singapore dollar would appreciate against the US dollar but not by the full amount. If a country does most of its trade with one major partner then keeping the currency fixed to that partner's currency might be desirable as it ensures stability in purchasing power for the majority of its trade. However, for a country, such as Singapore, which has a diversified pattern of trade, it makes more sense to monitor movements in the local currency against foreign currencies in some proportion to their importance as markets for exports or sources of imports.

In contrast to other major currencies, such as the euro, the pound sterling or the Japanese yen, which are largely allowed to float in the foreign exchange market, Singapore's basket currency or the trade-weighted Singapore dollar (TWS$) is only allowed to float within a policy band, determined by Singapore's central bank, the Monetary Authority of Singapore or MAS. On the other hand, unlike the Hong Kong dollar, which is tightly fixed to the US dollar at 7.8 Hong Kong dollars to the greenback, the use of a policy band allows market forces to determine the exchange rate to some degree and as a means of absorbing short-term market volatility, but without the volatility which might result if the currency were to float freely.

Finally, the policy band itself is adjusted from time to time and is allowed to "crawl" as circumstances change in the international arena and at home. E.g., the band may be set to appreciate the TWS$ by a certain amount over the next six months in line with the expected performance of the economy but in the intervening period news about underlying economic fundamentals, such as the rate of consumer price inflation or economic growth, may suggest a slower appreciation would be better. So the exchange rate is allowed to "crawl" towards the target rate rather than adjust immediately thus allowing more flexibility to policymakers to change their mind as economic conditions change and preventing the TWS$ from becoming "misaligned" or too strong or too weak.

The Formulation of Monetary Policy

In order to decide on the optimum or best path for the TWS$, the MAS will calculate several hypothetical exchange rate policy paths or scenarios. To help with the complex calculations involved they are able to call upon the Monetary Model of Singapore (MMS) which is a mathematical representation of the Singapore macro-economy involving more than 200 equations, including its trade and financial dealings with the rest of the world. This model is not available to the general public but by all accounts is a good representation of how the economy works and tracks past data well.

The experiments begin by making certain assumptions or forecasts about key variables relevant to monetary policy, such as the likely rates of economic growth in Singapore's major trading partners, such as the USA, Japan and European Union, as well as in Singapore's other trading partners in the Asian region. This will determine how fast Singapore's exports will grow. Also important is what is expected to happen to consumer price inflation, both within Singapore itself and in Singapore's trading partners, who might transmit their own domestic inflation to Singapore through rises in Singapore's import prices. Other forecasts might include commodity prices, such as petroleum or foodstuffs, or the foreign demand for particular goods that Singapore exports, such as electronics and pharmaceuticals, or the number of foreign tourists expected by the Singapore Tourism Board.

In order to choose the best exchange rate policy path from the alternative policy scenarios generated by the MMS, the MAS also seeks advice from sectoral specialists, such as business and finance analysts, conducts interviews with leading companies in the public and private sector and calls upon a range of other consultants. Then a particular policy path will be chosen for the exchange rate to ensure price stability over the medium term and this policy stance will be announced to the outside world.

Monetary Policy Communication

Until as recently as 2000, the MAS did not communicate its policy on the exchange rate to the public but, in common with other central banks in the world, it was increasingly recognized that greater transparency in monetary policy is essential to reduce the unpredictability of monetary policy and to prevent misunderstanding by the private sector and, thus, to reinforce the effectiveness of monetary policy.

Since 2000 there have been 3 main channels of communication between the MAS and the public at large. First, there is the release every 6 months in April and in October of the Monetary Policy Statement (MPS) which gives some indication of the main features of the BBC exchange rate system, such as the expected path of the TWS$ over the medium term, the slope of the policy band (rate of exchange rate appreciation) and its mid-point for the period ahead.

Figure 1 shows this information released during the MPS of April 2006 when the MAS re-affirmed its policy of a modest and gradual appreciation of the TWS$, including the expected path of the exchange rate from April to October 2006. This policy stance had been in place since April 2004. Note that there is not full transparency here about the width of the policy band (no band is shown) and the weights used to calculate the basket TWS$ itself. Professional observers can make quite good guesses about these things from past data but not giving away all the details allows the MAS some room to surprise the market on a day-to-day basis by intervening in the foreign exchange market itself to buy or sell the local currency in exchange for foreign currency, and may act as a deterrent to speculation against

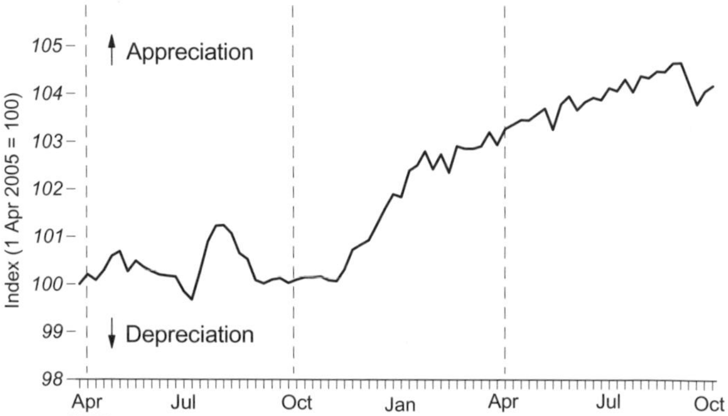

Source: Monetary Authority of Singapore.

Figure 1: The monetary policy statement and the TWS$ April 2006

the Singapore dollar which might arise if speculators knew exactly what the MAS would do in any given circumstances.

Although the MPS is the most important communication tool used by MAS to explain its monetary policy to the outside world, closed door briefings are also given to the Singapore media and private sector analysts coinciding with the release of the MPS and it publishes its *Macroeconomic Review* twice a year in April and October in conjunction with the release of the MPS. The *Macroeconomic Review* contains a more in-depth analysis of recent macroeconomic developments in the Singapore and global economies, the outlook for the next year or two and the rationale behind the policy decisions conveyed in the MPS.[2]

Implementation of Monetary Policy

There are two aspects to the implementation of monetary policy in Singapore: management of the exchange rate (TWS$) and management of domestic banking liquidity through money market operations.

The Singapore exchange rate regime is a managed float. The Singapore dollar is not left to float freely in the foreign exchange market but is managed, although only within a policy band and not as tightly as a fixed currency such as the Hong Kong dollar. Managing the exchange rate is a 24 hour operation and is carried out through intervention in the foreign exchange market. The basic principles are shown in Fig. 2, where an imaginary policy band for the TWS$ is drawn without slope (horizontal) for simplicity. Essentially, if the upper part of the TWS$ band is breached, the MAS will sell the Singapore dollar in the foreign exchange market in exchange for foreign currency, usually the US dollar. This action depreciates the TWS$ back towards the center of the band. On the other hand, if the lower part of the band is breached, the MAS will buy the Singapore dollar

[2] MAS also gives presentations to teachers and students and publishes educational material through its monographs on "Singapore's Exchange Rate Policy", its "Economics Explorer" pamphlets and Staff Papers. These materials, together with the bi-annual Macroeconomic Review are available online at mas.gov.sg.

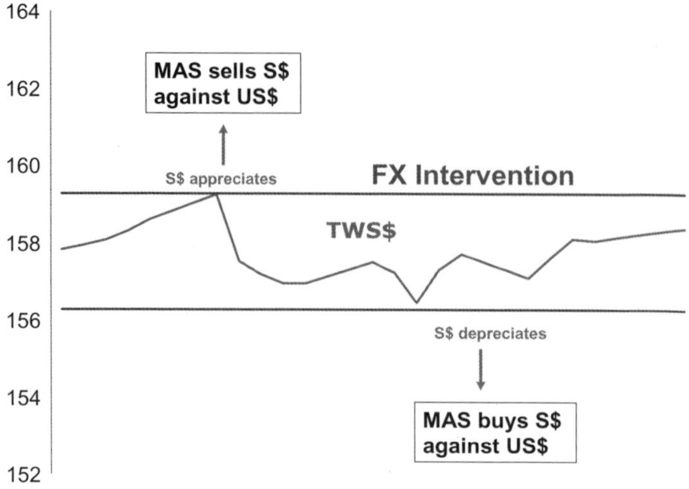

Source: Monetary Authority of Singapore.

Figure 2: Managing the trade-weighted Singapore dollar exchange rate index

with its reserves of foreign currency to appreciate it and bring it back into the band. Within the band itself there is no need for intervention and the TWS$ is determined by market forces. However, these are not mechanical rules and MAS may intervene within the band if, e.g., it believes that there is excessive volatility due to manipulation by speculative funds, or to act early to prevent strong momentum building up and pushing the TWS$ outside the band.

Although, as we shall see below, the MAS does not attempt to determine interest rates, which are largely set by money market supply and demand, the central bank does carry out money market operations which will affect liquidity in the domestic banking system and short-term interest rates. E.g., if there is too little liquidity in the money markets, the MAS could buy Singapore Government Securities (SGS) on the open market and in exchange provide liquidity to the banking system; and if there is too much liquidity it can sell SGS and thereby withdraw liquidity from the banking system. In this way the MAS can neutralize large inflows or outflows from the banking system and excessive volatility in interest rates. E.g., when liquidity is drained from the banking system by government budget surpluses, or from a rise in CPF contributions net of withdrawals. In this way money market operations by the MAS can inject back the same amount of liquidity into the money market and keep domestic interest rates stable.

The MAS may also want to neutralize or sterilize the effect on the money market of its own foreign exchange intervention to keep the TWS$ within its policy band (as described above). In this case it offsets the fall (rise) in the Singapore dollar due to its foreign exchange market activity with an opposite money market operation so as to leave the quantity of Singapore dollars constant.

Another motive for money market intervention is to make sure that there is sufficient liquidity in the domestic banking system to satisfy the banks' demand for cash balances to meet their intra-day settlements amongst themselves and with the central bank, since all banks in Singapore have to maintain cash reserves at the MAS interest free equal to 3 percent of their liabilities. MAS does this by offering discount or lending facilities on a daily basis.[3]

THE RATIONALE BEHIND SINGAPORE'S MONETARY POLICY

Traditional Monetary Policy

By choosing an exchange rate-centered monetary policy Singapore foregoes the use of traditional monetary policy for all intents and purposes. In other countries, such as Australia, Japan, the United Kingdom and in the European Monetary Union, their central banks will effect monetary policy by changing monetary aggregates, such as the broad measure of the money supply, M2, to try to influence local interest rates by buying and selling government securities in the open market (open-market operations).

---

[3] MAS' End-of-Day Liquidity Facility enables banks to cover their debits that may arise from end-of-day cheque-clearing positions. An Intra-Day Liquidity Facility allows Primary Dealers to borrow intra-day funds and Primary Dealers can also borrow twice a day through the MAS' Standing Facility.

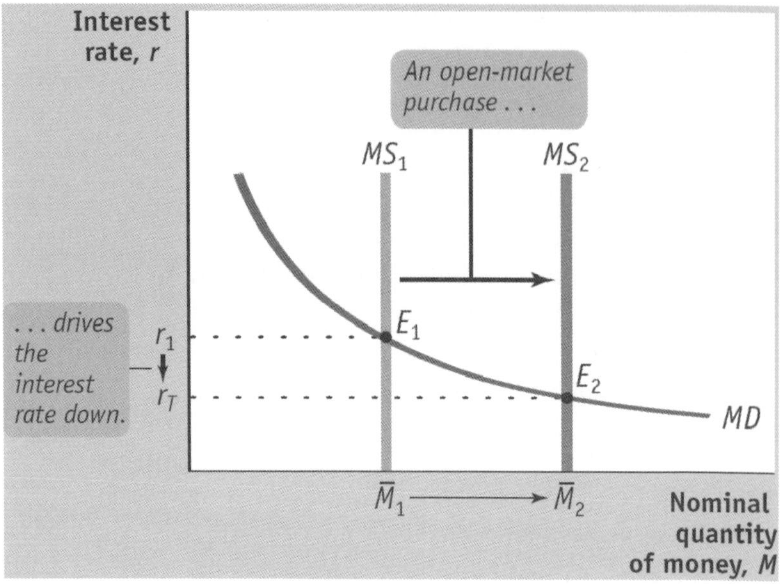

Figure 3: Traditional monetary policy

Figure 3 describes this process using the US Federal Reserve (the US central bank) for illustration. The MD curve shows the demand for money by domestic residents as determined by their need to hold money balances to finance their daily transactions and the interest rate, which represents the opportunity cost of holding money in zero or low interest earning accounts when the same money could be deposited in a higher interest savings account or used to purchase government or corporate bonds. Of course by moving money into a savings account there is a loss of liquidity since there will usually be financial penalties for early withdrawal, and buying bonds entails a financial risk which holding money normally does not.

The interest rate (r) on the vertical axis thus acts as the price of money in the sense that the higher it is, the less incentive there is for the general public to hold their money in non-interest earning accounts, so the demand for money (MD) is a negative function of r. Now if the Federal Reserve can change that part of the supply of money in the economy (MS) over which it has some control (the monetary base), it can effectively change interest rates in the economy, given the demand for money MD.

Suppose the Federal Reserve wants to stimulate the economy because it is worried that it might fall into recession, it could buy short-term government bonds (US Treasury bills) in the open market (open market operations), thereby increasing the amount of money held by the banking system (banks' cash balances) and enabling them to expand their lending to firms and consumers, and the stock of money in the economy would rise from MS_1 to MS_2.[4] As a result, the interest rate would fall from r_1 to r_T and cheaper money would encourage firms and consumers to borrow more to finance their investment and consumption expenditures and stimulate the economy. If the Federal Reserve was worried about inflationary pressures it could do the opposite and buy on the open market and thereby contract the money supply, raise the cost of borrowing, and reduce spending in the economy.

In this way a central bank, such as the Federal Reserve, can stimulate or contract the economy by altering the money supply (MS) directly or indirectly by targeting the interest rate r, although it cannot fix both the quantity and the price of money simultaneously, since setting one determines the other automatically as Fig. 3 implies. Since the early 1990s, the Federal Reserve has tended to focus its day-to day monetary policy on targeting the Federal Funds rate (FFR) or the rate at which the US banks lend to each other. Since other interest rates in the economy tend to move in tandem with the FFR (see Fig. 4), this effectively means that the Federal Reserve can influence other interest rates in the economy, such as the Prime Lending Rate and the 30 Year Mortgage Rate. Note that if targeting the FFR is insufficient to move the economy in the right direction, the Federal Reserve, in common with other central banks, can simply offer to lend more to the banks, and in some cases, bail them out completely. A good example of this is the recent sub-prime mortgage crisis when

[4] This is the textbook money multiplier process whereby the overall supply of money in the economy is expanded by a multiple of the original increase in base money through the process of financial intermediation.

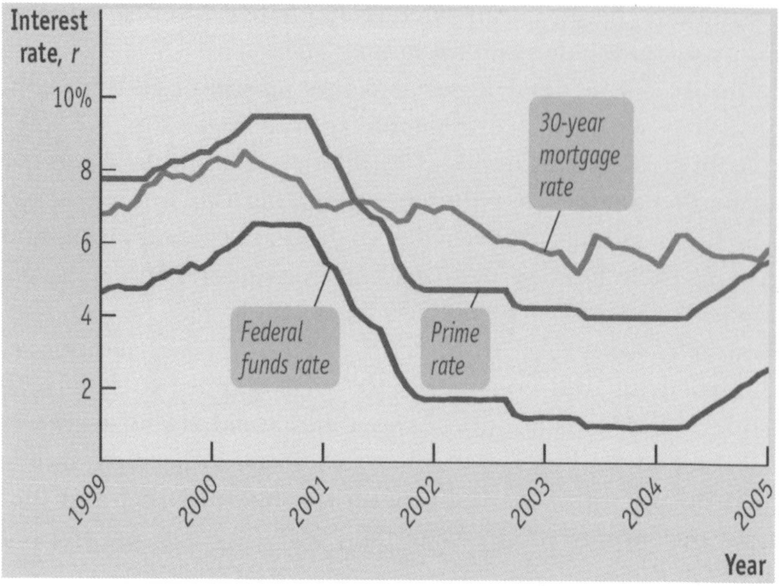

Figure 4: The Federal Reserve moves interest rates

all the major central banks substantially increased the loans they were willing to make to financial institutions and the UK government took the extreme step of taking Northern Rock, one of the banks in trouble, into national ownership.

Why is Singapore's Monetary Policy Exchange-Rate Centered?

Why does Singapore's central bank not adopt a conventional monetary policy as described above? The answer to this question is found in the rather unique characteristics of the Singapore economy, as well as its economic history.

To begin with, Singapore has always been a very open economy, meaning that the ratio of its exports and imports to Gross Domestic Product (GDP) is extremely high by international standards. As shown in Fig. 5, the sum of Singapore's exports and imports is in excess of 3 times its GDP. This follows from the fact that Singapore imposes

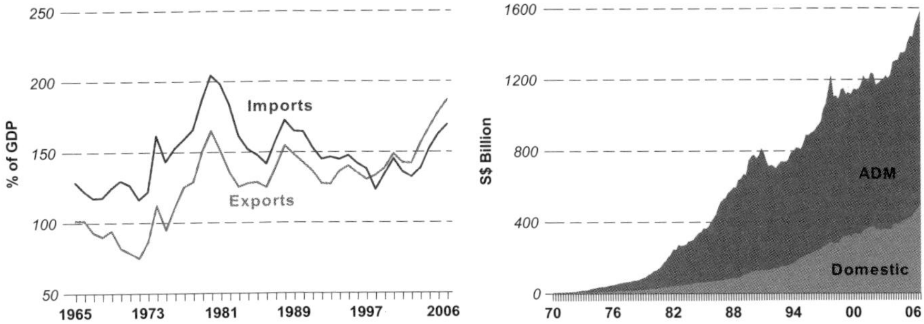

Source: Monetary Authority of Singapore.

Figure 5: Singapore's openness to trade and capital flows

negligible tariffs and quotas on imports from the rest of the world, and since it has little by way of natural resources it must import most of what it needs and export to pay for it. Other countries in the world are also very open to trade, such as Malaysia and Hong Kong, but what singles Singapore out is its very high import content of domestic expenditure and exports. Out of every dollar spent in Singapore about 50 cents goes to foreigners in payment for imports and a large proportion of the value of a good exported from Singapore consists of imported intermediate inputs. Out of every dollar of refined petroleum exported from Singapore, approximately 90 cents is accounted for by imported crude oil.

The implication of this is that Singapore is a classic price-taker in world markets since it is too small as an exporter or importer to have any discernable impact on international prices. So domestic prices are largely determined by world prices for a given exchange rate. The price of Thai rice in Singapore's supermarkets, e.g., is essentially the Thai export price in the Thai currency — the baht — converted into Singapore dollars at the prevailing exchange rate.

What the MAS has done, since 1981, has been to turn this import dependence into a virtue by taking advantage of the powerful link between the exchange rate, import prices, and domestic prices. If, for instance, consumer price inflation is rising in Singapore, as in the first quarter of 2008, and the MAS wants to bring it down, rather than tightening monetary policy by raising interest rates, as would occur in a country using traditional monetary policy, instead it appreciates the TWS$ by buying the S$ in the foreign exchange market, as described earlier. Because domestic prices are largely determined by world prices for a given exchange rate, the appreciation of the TWS$ effectively lowers import prices and, subsequently, wholesale and consumer prices, as the effects of the appreciation pass-through to the domestic economy.

Experiments using the MMS have shown that the impact of exchange rate policy on GDP, exports and the consumer price index is significantly stronger than an equivalent change in the interest rate. In the jargon of central banks, the exchange rate is a good (controllable) intermediate target or instrument and bears a stable and predictable relationship with price stability as the ultimate target of monetary policy over the medium term. In other words, Singapore's exchange rate-centered monetary policy may have been born out of necessity and is certainly unorthodox, but it works!

A second factor determining the choice of monetary policy in Singapore since 1981 is Singapore's openness to international capital flows. Foreign exchange controls and restrictions on inflows and outflows of capital were removed in 1978 and Singapore has always adopted an open-arms approach to investment by foreign multinational corporations (MNCs), providing they are export-oriented. Again, this is not unique to Singapore, but what makes Singapore different is the very close relationship between the domestic banking system and the substantially larger offshore Asian Dollar Market or ADM (see Fig. 4).[5]

What this means is that if there is any discrepancy between domestic interest rates in Singapore and those in the offshore market, banks in Singapore can move their funds quickly offshore to earn a higher return. There is, in essence, almost perfect capital mobility and

[5] The ADM is a market where the banks in Singapore which are licensed to deal in the ADM can lend and borrow in a foreign (offshore) currency, usually the US dollar. Even if the transaction is in another currency such as the yen, it is still referred to, by convention as the Asian Dollar Market.

substitutability between domestic (onshore) and foreign (offshore) financial assets. The consequence of this is that interest rates in Singapore are largely determined by world money markets, including the ADM. Singapore is simply too small, in the financial sense, and too open, in the trading sense, to set its own interest rates. If the MAS decided to copy the monetary policy of the Federal Reserve and lower interest rates to stimulate a recovery from a recession, all that would happen is that money would flow out of Singapore's domestic banks into offshore bank accounts where interest rates have not fallen. In terms of Fig. 3, this outflow would automatically contract the money supply in Singapore back to MS_1 and the original attempt by the monetary Authority to lower r to r_T, would be thwarted. The MAS knows this and does not even try to influence interest rates beyond the minor smoothing discussed earlier.

The choice of an exchange rate-centered monetary policy for Singapore is also supported by economic theory which suggests that economic policymakers are faced with three desirable but, at times contradictory, macroeconomic objectives, which cannot be achieved simultaneously. This is known as the "Policy trilemma" or "impossible trinity". The three objectives are exchange rate management to stabilize the currency, the ability to carry out domestic monetary policy by targeting domestic interest rates or the money supply (traditional monetary policy or monetary autonomy), and free capital mobility in order to integrate with global financial markets. Policymakers can choose two of the three objectives but have to decide which third objective to give up.

Figure 6 illustrates the policy trilemma for Singapore. The corners of the triangle show the policy goals just described. Unfortunately, at most only two can be achieved at the same time. E.g., if Singapore wishes to achieve exchange rate stability by managing its currency (managed floating) and simultaneously keep its capital market open (free capital mobility), it will have to sacrifice traditional monetary policy or monetary autonomy. Any attempt to use monetary policy would drive the local interest rate away from world rates and in an open capital market it would be forced back into line with world rates. By contrast, the USA can continue to use domestic monetary

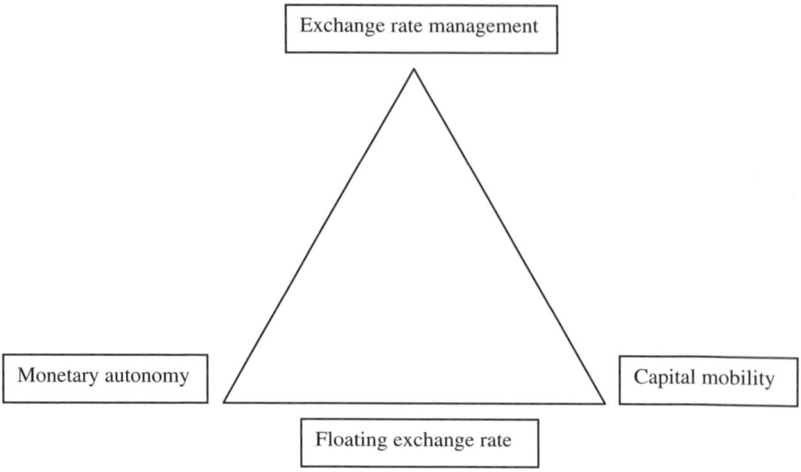

Source: Mankiw, Quah and Wilson (2008).

Figure 6: The policy trilemma for Singapore

policy to expand or contract the economy and at the same time keep its capital market open but has to sacrifice exchange rate management as a major objective of macroeconomic policy and let its currency float freely. In September 1998, during the Asian financial crisis, Malaysia decided to fix its currency — the ringgit — to the US dollar, and since it wanted to continue using traditional monetary policy to stimulate a recovery in the domestic economy, it was forced to abandon free capital mobility and introduce capital and currency controls.

Thus, because managed floating is thought to be more effective in achieving Singapore's domestic macroeconomic goals than traditional monetary policy and Singapore wants to keep the capital market as open as possible, traditional monetary policy is abandoned in favor of exchange rate management, as the quotation from former Finance Minister, Richard Hu, at the beginning of the chapter confirms.[6]

[6] Another way of thinking about this is that since monetary policy in Singapore is targeted at the exchange rate, which involves changing the stock of Singapore dollars whenever the MAS intervenes to manage the currency, the MAS cannot simultaneously target either money supply aggregates (such as M1 or M2) or the interest rate.

HAS MONETARY POLICY IN SINGAPORE BEEN SUCCESSFUL?

There is no doubt that monetary policy in Singapore has been very successful since 1981 and has enabled the Republic to cope with external shocks. Figure 7 plots the TWS$ since 1980.[7] As can be seen, the basket measure of the currency has generally appreciated over the longer run, due principally to Singapore's strong growth performance. But there have been periods when the exchange rate has needed to adjust to cope with upturns and downturns in the economy, often stemming from external causes.

In 1985, e.g., Singapore experienced its first major recession since independence in 1965. To speed up recovery and help export

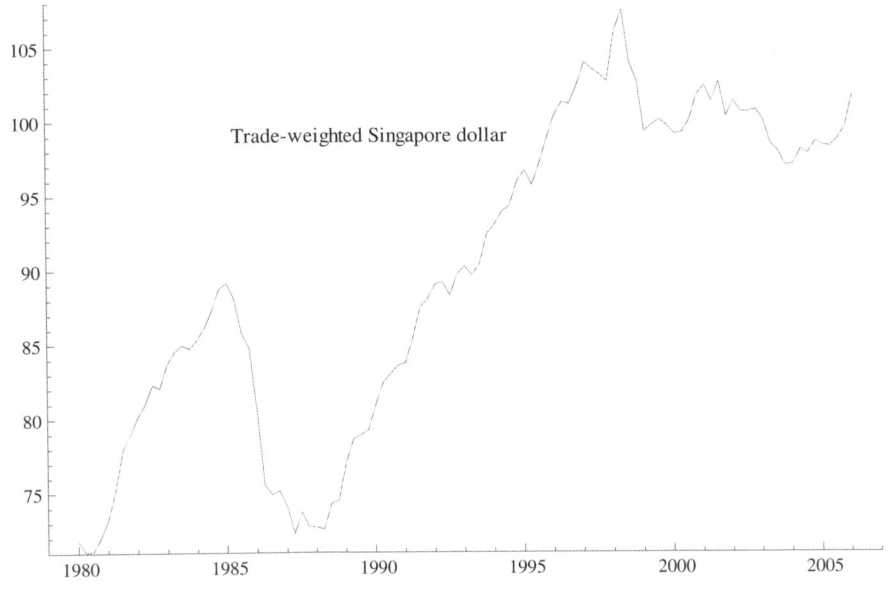

Source: International Monetary Fund, *International Financial Statistics*.

Figure 7: The trade-weighted Singapore dollar exchange rate (1980–2006)

[7] Note that this is not the MAS' own TWS$, which is kept a secret, but a similar one calculated with data from the International Monetary Fund.

competitiveness, the MAS allowed the TWS$ to depreciate, but much of the adjustment came from government-determined cost cuts, including a 15 percentage point cut in the employers' CPF contribution rate, and cuts in wages. The economy recovered quickly from the recession and the following period up to the Asian financial crisis of 1997–98 was a golden age of strong growth and falling unemployment. To offset the build-up of inflationary pressures during this period, the MAS allowed the TWS$ to appreciate, thus lowering import costs so that rapid economic growth of about 8 percent per year did not lead to excessive inflationary pressures.

The Asian financial crisis, beginning with the rapid depreciation of the Thai baht in July 1997, spread to Singapore because of Singapore's openness to international trade and capital flows. The TWS$ initially appreciated because other currencies were falling faster, but the MAS eased monetary policy by allowing the Singapore dollar to depreciate and widened its policy band to give more room to the market to move the currency down. Thus, again, monetary policy through the BBC exchange rate mechanism helped Singapore to weather the storm. In fact, Singapore escaped relatively unscathed from the crisis.

The next two crises were of a different nature. In 2001 there was a slowdown in the global electronics market following the bursting of the dot.com bubble. Export-oriented Singapore was badly hit. Monetary policy, which had returned after the Asian financial crisis to a modest appreciation of the TWS$, was now shifted to a neutral stance. This did not save Singapore from negative economic growth but together with another cost-cutting package, it certainly helped. Monetary policy was also eased following the outbreak of the SARS crisis in 2003.

Since the second half of 2003 the Singapore economy has enjoyed sustained strong growth and job creation and, accordingly, monetary policy has been tightened gradually using the "crawl" feature of the BBC principle. With the sharp increase in imported inflation in the first part of 2008 and continuing strength in the economy, it will be interesting to see if there is a change in monetary policy in November 2008.

Apart from helping the economy adjust to external shocks, monetary policy in Singapore is also designed to reduce volatility in the Singapore dollar exchange rate. On the whole, the TWS$ has been more stable than other major currencies, thus justifying the "basket" feature of the BBC exchange rate system. The volatility of the TWS$, as measured by its standard deviation, was 1.40 percent between the first quarter of 1981 and the first quarter of 2007, compared to 3.29 percent and 4.45 percent for the US dollar and Japanese yen, respectively. Moreover, on a bilateral basis, the Singapore dollar has been less volatile against the US dollar, the yen and the euro than these currencies have been against each other. Counterfactual experiments both before and after the Asian financial crisis also confirm that Singapore's managed floating exchange rate regime has coped well with exchange rate volatility when compared with other countries' exchange rate regimes and a number of hypothetical regimes, such as fixing to the US dollar (Wilson and Ng, 2008).

Most important of all, monetary policy in Singapore has been able to deliver low consumer price inflation, which averaged 1.7 percent between January 1981 and May 2007, and this has provided a stable macroeconomic environment for both producers and consumers. Apart from the first oil shock in the mid-1970s, which was global in its impact, Singapore's inflation rate compares very favorably with weighted average inflation in its Organization of Economic Cooperation and Development (OECD) trading partners (Fig. 8). If there were a

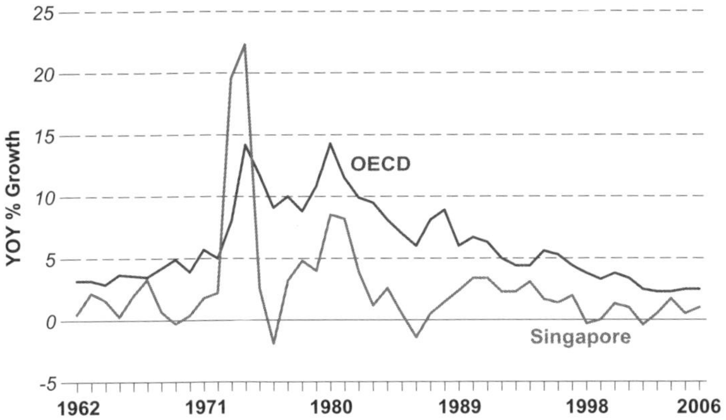

Source: Monetary Authority of Singapore.

Figure 8: Inflation in Singapore compared to the OECD countries

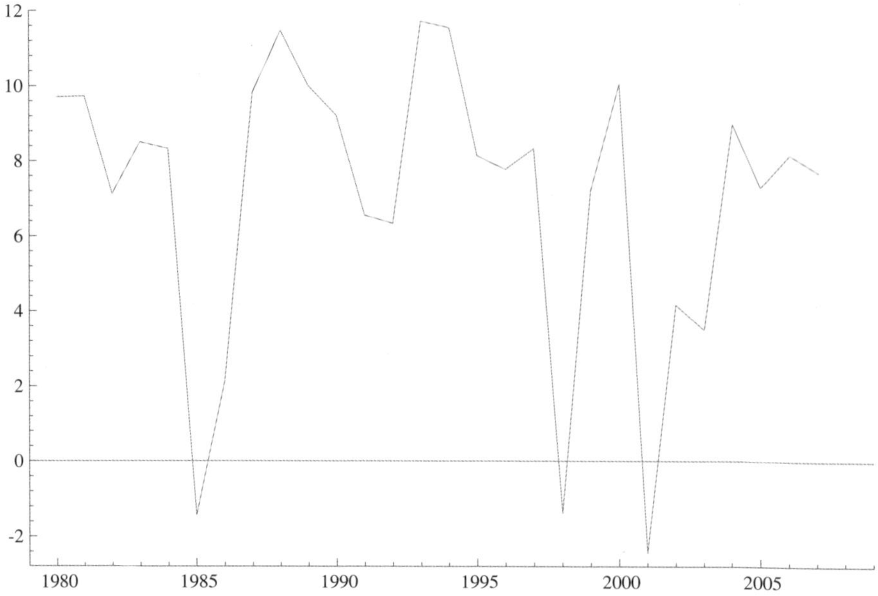

Source: Department of Statistics, Singapore.

Figure 9: Real GDP growth in Singapore (%)

Champions League in central banking, MAS would certainly have qualified!

Moreover, price stability has not been at the expense of economic growth, given rise to prolonged periods of high unemployment, or in general caused problems for exports and the balance of payments. Figure 9 plots annual GDP growth in Singapore since 1980. Despite a number of external shocks to the economy, as described above, Singapore's GDP grew, on average, by 7 percent per year between 1980 and 2007. Notice that whilst the Singapore economy went into recession (negative growth) in 1985–86, 1998–99, and 2001–02, the economy has always recovered quickly, partly due to good monetary policy. Unemployment, therefore, rises during economic downturns but falls soon after and, on average, unemployment has been quite low (Fig. 10).

As a general rule, countries which grow fast and undergo a period of rapid economic growth often find that excess demand for goods

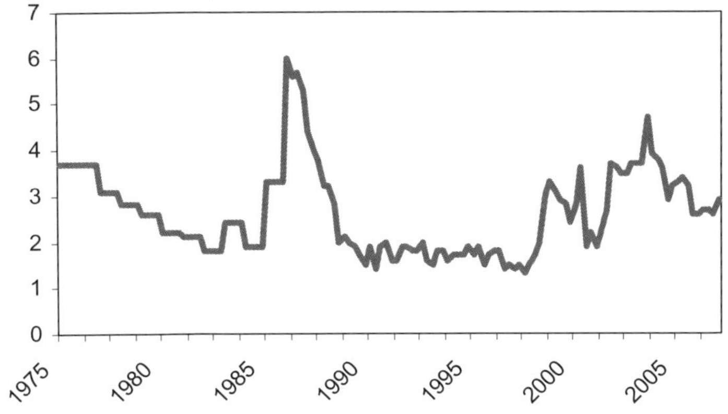

Source: Department of Statistics, Singapore.

Figure 10: Unemployment in Singapore (%)

and services in an open economy tends to spill over into deficits in the balance of payments as imports are sucked in faster than exports can be produced. Also, when there are inflationary pressures and the MAS tightens monetary policy by intervening in the foreign exchange market to appreciate the Singapore dollar, this can raise the prices of Singapore's exports to foreign countries and make Singapore firms less competitive. Whether this has in fact happened is still a little controversial and difficult to measure, since the exchange rate is only one of a number of factors which determine export competitiveness (Abeysinghe and Wilson, 2002). Those companies in Singapore which are very price competitive in foreign markets but do not benefit much from a fall in import costs when the Singapore dollar is appreciated will be most affected. But as far as the current account and overall balance of payments are concerned, Singapore has recorded consistent and sizeable surpluses as a percent of national income since 1981 (Table 1).

Monetary Policy Does Not Work Alone

Of course, monetary policy does not work in a vacuum and cannot be given all the credit for Singapore's successful economic performance

Table 1: The Singapore Balance of Payments (1980–2006)

	Annual averages				
% of National income	1980–85	1986–1989	1990–1996	1997–2000	2001–2006
Current account balance	–5.6	5.1	12.7	21.9	25.6
Overall balance	7.1	6.3	10.1	5.8	7.3

Source: Monetary Authority of Singapore.

since 1981. Luckily Singapore has strong supporting macroeconomic institutions which ensure a good degree of consistency in policy and reinforce the credibility of its monetary policy. In particular, because the government generally runs a budget surplus and does not accumulate foreign debt, there is no need for the MAS to finance government debt so it can concentrate on its own monetary objectives. In many other countries in the world, especially developing countries, the central bank is diverted from its main function by the need to finance the government's excessive spending or revenue shortfall.

Secondly, in spite of the fact that the Singapore government exerts a significant amount of control over the economy through Statutory Boards and government-linked companies, it has always encouraged market-oriented activity and resisted the temptation to protect firms and workers from changes in the global economy. The labor and capital markets are relatively flexible, in the sense that wages and profits can be adjusted downwards when the economy goes into a downturn, and economic policy in Singapore since the mid-1960s has always been pro-growth, pro-international trade, and welcoming to foreign investment (Peebles and Wilson, 2005).

Finally, Singapore has a good international reputation for corporate governance. Corruption in the government and the Civil Service is extremely rare, the financial system is well-regulated and financial institutions based in Singapore adhere closely to international best practices. This ensures that when financial crises do occur, as with the recent sub-prime mortgage market collapse, Singapore is generally in a good position to absorb the shocks which result. Singapore also has a substantial quantity of foreign exchange reserves to fall back on during periods of crisis.

CONCLUSION

In this chapter we have looked at Singapore's unusual, but highly successful, monetary policy since 1981. As with other central banks, the imperative of the MAS is to preserve the purchasing power of the Singapore dollar in international markets. Since 1981, Singapore's monetary policy has been centered on the exchange rate with the primary objective of ensuring domestic price stability as an anchor for macroeconomic stability in general and a sound basis for sustainable economic growth.

The exchange rate is managed against a trade-weighted basket of currencies but is allowed to float within a policy band determined by the MAS and the policy stance is adjusted from time to time through a "crawl" mechanism. A particular policy path is identified twice a year which will ensure price stability over the medium term and this "policy stance" is then communicated to the general public in order to obtain feedback, prevent misunderstanding and generally to reinforce the credibility and effectiveness of monetary policy. Because of Singapore's extreme openness to international trade and capital flows and its desire to "manage" the currency to some degree, the MAS effectively gives up control of domestic interest rates, which are set by international financial markets, although it does engage in daily money market operations to reduce excessive volatility in interest rates and ensure that there is sufficient liquidity in the local banking system.

There is no doubt that despite its unorthodoxy, monetary policy in Singapore has been very successful since 1981 in helping the economy to adjust to periodic economic shocks, such as the Asian financial crisis of 1997–98. It has also delivered a stable currency, low and stable consumer price inflation without sacrificing economic growth and employment, and has avoided balance of payments crises.

The success of monetary policy in Singapore has also been helped by a flexible labor market and strong supporting institutions which have ensured consistency in economic policy and provided an environment conducive to rapid export and FDI-led economic growth. The financial system has, by and large, been well-regulated and a high savings policy has provided a large and growing pool of foreign exchange reserves to reinforce the credibility of exchange rate policy and provide the means for the MAS to actively engage in the foreign exchange market to manage the Singapore dollar.

END NOTES

Abeysinghe, T and P Wilson (2002). International Competitiveness. In *The Singapore Economy in the 21st Century: Issues and Strategies*. Chng, MK, W Hui, A Koh, K Lim and B Rao (eds.), Singapore: McGraw-Hill.

Khor, HE *et al.* (2007). Managed float exchange rate system: The Singapore experience. *The Singapore Economic Review*, 52(1), pp. 7–25.

Mankiw, G, E Quah and P Wilson (2008). *Principles of Economics*: An Asian Edition, Cengage Learning.

Monetary Authority of Singapore (2007). Monetary Policy Operations in Singapore (available online at mas.gov.sg).

Parrado, E (2004). Singapore's Unique Monetary Policy: How Does it Work? Monetary Authority of Singapore, Staff Papers, No. 31.

Peebles, G and P Wilson (2002). *Economic Growth and Development in Singapore: Past and Future*. Cheltenham, UK: Edward Elgar.

Peebles, G and P Wilson (2005). Don't frighten the horses — the political economy of Singapore's foreign exchange rate regime since 1981. Singapore Centre for Applied and Policy Economics (SCAPE), Working Paper 2005/06.

Wilson, P and H Ng (2008). Managing Exchange Rate Volatility: A Comparative Counterfactual Analysis of Singapore 1994 to 2003. *The Singapore Economic Review* (forthcoming).

Chapter

5

Capital Accumulation, Capital-Output Ratio and Total Factor Productivity in Singapore

Sng Hui Ying

INTRODUCTION

Capital, together with labor, land and technology, are the key factors of production. Various growth theories relate the growth of capital to the growth of output. In Rostow's growth model, an increase of investment rate to 10% or more is necessary before growth can gather enough momentum to take-off. In the Harrod-Domar model, the growth rate of national output is equal to the growth rate of capital. In Lim's S-Curve hypothesis (1996, 2004), the rapid accumulation of physical capital is an important driver behind the superlative growth of the Newly Industrializing Economies (NIEs). De Long and Summers (1991, 1993) have also shown that investment in machinery and equipment has a strong association with growth.

However, statistical evidences on the importance of capital accumulation in causing GDP growth are mixed. Several studies on the causality between capital accumulation and GDP growth have been conducted. While studies using panel data often produce results that disagree that it is capital growth that causes output growth (Blomstrom *et al.*, 1996; Podrecca and Carmeci, 2001), studies on individual countries show that the causal relationship between investment and growth is country-specific and may run in either direction (Ghali and Al-Mutawa, 1999; Hatemi-J and Irandoust, 2002).

Singapore experienced very rapid increase in GDP between 1960s and 1990s on the back on sharp increases in factor inputs. However, Krugman (1994) and Young (1995) dismiss the spectacular rise of Singapore's GDP by emphasizing that Singapore's Total Factor Productivity (TFP) growth was negligible and that the high economic growth was only driven by resource accumulation. Krugman even predicts that Singapore could face a "Soviet-style" growth collapse. This Chapter disagrees with Krugman and Young, and takes the view that a sharp increase in capital accumulation during the development process of a developing country is necessary to fuel current and future economic growth.

This Chapter postulates that capital accumulation of an economy follows an S-Curve as the economy develops. The hypothesis suggests that a NIE would experience rapid accumulation of capital, and this rate of capital growth would slowly taper off as the economy develops. This sharp increase in capital accumulation is necessary to fuel further economic growth. It is further postulated that the growth rate of capital stock is likely to outpace that of GDP during the early phase of industrialization. As a result of this S-Curve of capital accumulation, the incremental capital-output ratio (ICOR) and the average capital-output ratio (ACOR) of the economy are likely to first increase, and then gradually decrease as the economy ascends the development ladder.

The outline of this Chapter is as follows: Section 1 puts forth the hypothesis of the S-Curve of capital accumulation and the probable patterns of capital-output ratios as an economy develops. Section 2 presents a case study of Singapore. Section 3 tests the long term causal relationship between Singapore's capital stock and GDP and found it to be positive and bi-directional. Section 4 revisits the issue of TFP growth and capital growth in Singapore.

1. HYPOTHESIS OF THE S-CURVE OF CAPITAL ACCUMULATION AND ITS IMPLIED CAPITAL-OUTPUT RATIO

1.1. S-Curve of Capital Accumulation

According to Lim's S-Curve hypothesis (1996, 2004), the development of an economy can be divided into 3 stages: Stage 1 (underdevelopment with low-income and slow growth), Stage 2 (rapid development with middle income and rapid growth), and Stage 3 (highly developed with high-income and slow growth).

If capital accumulation is strongly associated with output growth, then a Stage 1 economy is likely to have a low-level of per capita capital stock and a low-rate of capital accumulation. Rate of capital accumulation would gain momentum as the economy enters Stage 2 of economic development, and the level of per capita capital stock, increases. A Stage 3 economy would enjoy a high-level of per capita capital stock but its rate of capital accumulation, although is still positive, would gradually decline.

An underdeveloped Stage 1 economy is likely to have a low-level of per capita capital stock. This is intuitive as capital investment needs to be financed out of savings from income which is lacking in the poor countries. In addition, foreign investment is likely to be scarce in the absence of investment-conducive policies. Growth rate of per capita capital stock is also expected to be low since governments of developing countries often have limited tax-collecting and revenue-generating capabilities.

On the other hand, a Stage 2 NIE with its improving business environment, better property rights protection and a comparatively cheaper cost structure would attract both foreign and domestic direct investment. The influx of foreign investment would provide increased business opportunities to domestic producers, thereby inducing further domestic investment. Moreover, as the fiscal position of the government improves, the government would be able to invest more heavily in the development of physical infrastructure and human capital. It is further postulated that the growth rate of capital stock would outpace that of GDP during the early phase of industrialization.

A highly developed Stage 3 economy that has experienced continued capital accumulation over prolonged period would have a high-level of per capita capital stock. However, capital growth rate is likely to slow down due to diminishing returns of capital. In addition, the high-cost of production in the developed countries would lead to direct investment, especially those from the manufacturing sector, to flow to the cheaper developing countries.

The graphical representation of the time paths of capital stock and output level as an economy develops is shown in Fig. 1.

1.2. Time Path of Capital-Output Ratios

Due to a general lack of supply of capital and an excess supply of labor, an underdeveloped Stage 1 economy is likely to have low-levels of incremental capital-output ratio (ICOR = $\Delta K/\Delta Y$)

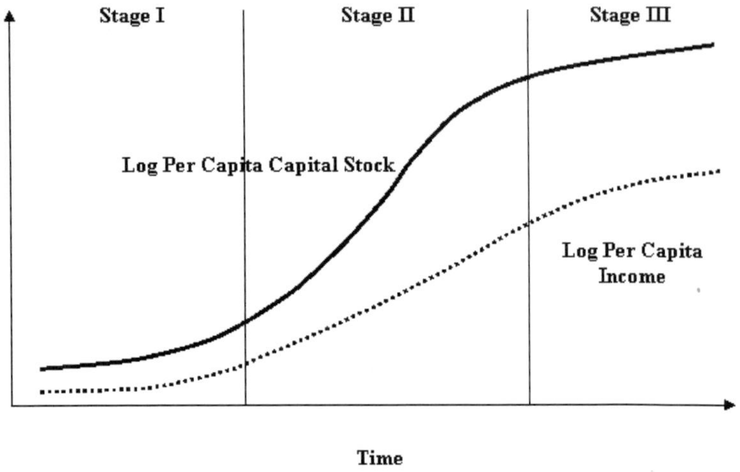

Figure 1: S-Curve of capital accumulation

and average capital-output ratio (ACOR = K/Y) (where K = capital stock, Y = GDP) as production processes are likely to be labor-intensive.

The NIE is likely to experience increasing ICOR and ACOR. Firstly, a rapidly developing economy is expected to undergo a period of rapid increase in capital investment. In the short to medium term, as the investment rate expands rapidly while the output growth lags behind, ICOR (= $(I/Y)/(\Delta Y/Y)$) will inevitably be pushed up. Secondly, as the excess labor in the economy is exhausted, production process has to become increasingly capital-intensive, and thus leading to higher ICOR. Thirdly, the government would be undertaking large-scale infrastructural projects which have higher levels of ICOR. As the NIE gradually matures into a developed economy, the rate of increase of ICOR will slow down, and the level of ICOR may even start to decline.

A highly-developed economy with its high-level of accumulated investment is likely to have a low investment rate. At the same time, the developed economy continues to reap the returns of earlier investment, especially those in infrastructure and buildings that have very long service lives. Thus, the ICOR of a developed economy is likely to be falling, albeit gradually, as the investment rate falls faster than the GDP growth rate. However, as the production processes adopted in a developed economy is of much higher capital intensity, the ICOR of the developed economy would be higher than that of an underdeveloped economy. As ICOR declines, ACOR would eventually stabilize or even decline.

The probable time paths of the ACOR and the ICOR over the development process of a country are given in Fig. 2.

2. SINGAPORE'S CAPITAL ACCUMULATION AND OUTPUT GROWTH

2.1. Estimation of Singapore's Capital Stock

Data on Singapore's capital stock are constructed from data on Gross Fixed Capital Formation (GFCF) at 2000 prices using the Perpetual

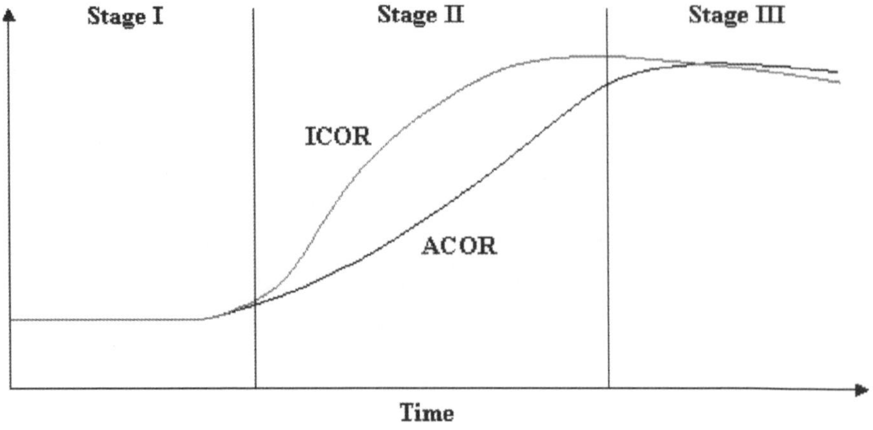

Figure 2: Probable time paths of capital-output ratios

Inventory Method (PIM).[1] Straight-line depreciation is assumed and the assumptions on the longevity of various categories of capital stock, ranging from 15 to 80 years, follow those used by the Singapore's Department of Statistics (DOS) in their computation of the capital stock of Singapore (Department of Statistics, 1997; OECD, 2001).[2]

2.2. Singapore's Capital Stock

Figure 3 presents the estimated net capital stock of Singapore from 1960–2006. The time path of Singapore's accumulation of capital stock concurs with the hypothesis of S-Curve of capital accumulation. The accumulation of capital got on a slow start during the early phase of the Singapore's economic development (low-level and low-growth of capital). The building up of capital gained momentum in late 1960s, signaling Singapore's entrance into a new phase of rapid

[1] The PIM accumulates past purchases of each asset type, and removes from the capital stock fixed assets that are scrapped upon reaching the end of their respective service lives.

[2] Details on the construction of the data series of the capital stock of Singapore can be found in Sng (2007).

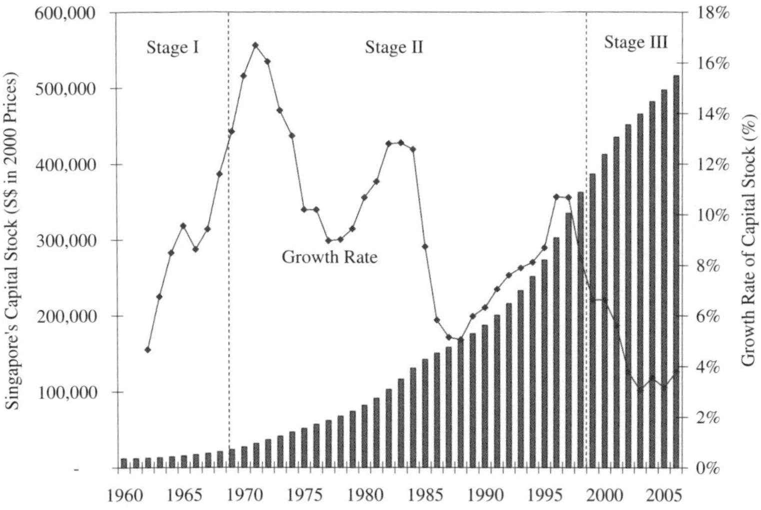

Source: Estimation using raw data from CEIC database.

Figure 3: Singapore's net capital stock (S$ in 2000 Prices), 1960–2005

industrialization (medium-level and high-growth of capital). The growth of capital stock appears to slow down since 1998 (high-level and low-growth of capital).

2.3. Capital Accumulation and Economic Development of Singapore

Singapore's per capita GDP has grown in tandem with the increase in the per capita capital stock over the years (see Fig. 4). In 1960, Singapore's per capita GDP and per capita capital stock were both very low at only S$4,080 and S$7,290, respectively. Singapore began its metamorphosis into a NIE from mid-1960s. And since mid-1960s to late-1990s, Singapore's per capita capital stock grew rapidly, so did its per capita GDP. However, it can be seen from Fig. 4 that the growth of both the per capita GDP and the per capita capital stock appear to be slowing down since late 1990s.

Table 1 shows that since the 1970s, the growth rates of per capita capital stock were consistently higher than that of the GDP.

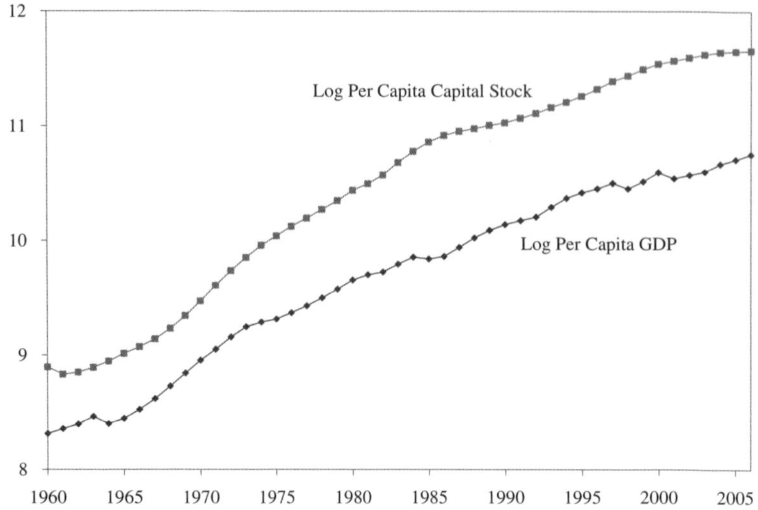

Source: Estimation using raw data from CEIC database.

Figure 4: Singapore's log per capita GDP and log per capita capital stock (S$ in 2000 Prices), 1960–2005

Table 1: Average annual growth rates of Singapore's per capita GDP and per capita capital stock (in 2000 Prices)

Year	Per Capita GDP (%)	Per Capita Capital Stock (%)
1960–1969	6.0	5.1
1970–1979	7.1	10.2
1980–1989	4.9	6.5
1990–1999	4.3	5.3
2000–2006	2.7	1.9
1960–2006	**5.4**	**6.2**

Source: Estimation using raw data from CEIC database.

This is in line with our proposition that the per capita capital stock of a NIE would rise faster than its per capita GDP. Furthermore, the difference between the two sets of growth rates narrowed as the time went by. This supports the proposition that the increase in GDP will catch up with that of capital stock during the later phase of development as the economy continues to reap benefits of earlier investments.

2.4. Singapore's Capital-Output Ratios

Figure 5 shows the variability of Singapore's ACOR over the period 1960–2006. Level of ACOR was rising steadily from less than 1.8 in early 1960s to about 2.8 in early 2000s. There were four prominent upsurges of the ACOR over the last 47 years, and they coincided with the recessionary years of Singapore: 1964, 1985, 1998 and 2001. During recession, output falls sharply while capital stock remains relatively stable resulting in an under-utilization of capital. This leads a sudden increase in ACOR, which is not representative.

It can be seen from Fig. 5 that Singapore's ACOR expanded rapidly in the first 20 years after Singapore attained independence in 1965. This is in line with the hypothesis of the S-Curve of capital accumulation: NIE would experience increasing ACOR (and ICOR) during the early stage of industrialization. The steady increase of the ACOR ran out

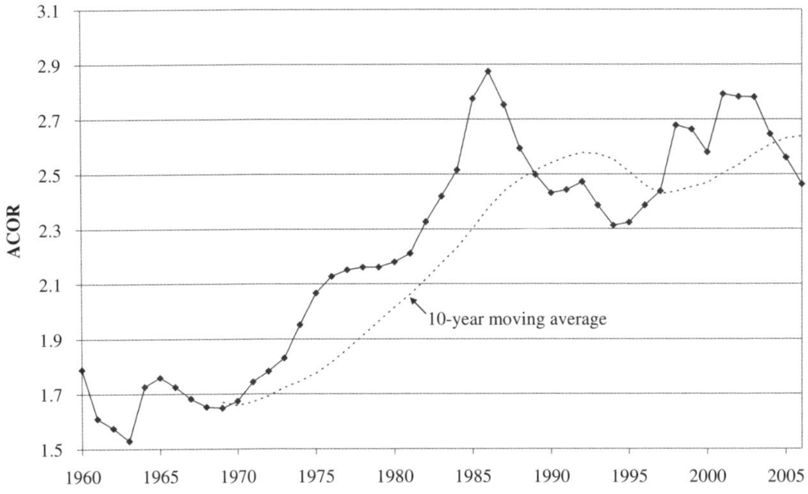

Source: Estimation using raw data from CEIC database.

Figure 5: Singapore's average capital-output ratio, 1960–2006

of steam in the late 1980s, and the ACOR was range-bound between 2.3 and 2.8 since 1988. The level of ACOR in 2006 was 2.5. Given Singapore's advanced stage of development, future level of ACOR is expected to hover around 2.6 and may even gradually decline.

3. GRANGER CAUSALITY BETWEEN SINGAPORE'S CAPITAL STOCK AND GDP

Granger Causality Bivariate Vector Error Correction Model (VECM) Test is used in this section to establish the causality between Singapore's capital stock (*K*) and GDP (*Y*). While the Augmented Dickey-Fuller (ADF) test shows that unit root exists in both the data series of K_t and Y_t, the first differences of K_t and Y_t are found to be stationary. The Johansen cointegration test shows that both K_t and Y_t are cointegrated, i.e., there exists a long-term equilibrium relationship between capital stock and GDP.

A Bivariate VECM is set up to establish the causality between capital stock and GDP:

$$\Delta Y_t = \mu + \theta(Y_{t-1} - \alpha - \beta K_{t-1}) + \sum \alpha_i \Delta K_{t-i} + \sum \beta_j \Delta Y_{t-j} + U_{yt}$$
$$\Delta K_t = \omega + \phi(Y_{t-1} - \alpha - \beta K_{t-1}) + \sum \gamma_i \Delta K_{t-i} + \sum \delta_j \Delta Y_{t-j} + U_{mt}$$

A lag of 1 period is found to minimize the value of the Akaike's Information Criteria (AIC). The VECM estimates are given as follows:

θ	−0.158*
ϕ	0.055**
$\Sigma\alpha_i$	−0.025
$\Sigma\delta_i$	0.341*

* denotes significance at 1 percent level
** at 5 percent level

The results of the VECM estimates show that there existed a positive and significant bi-directional long-term causal relationship between Singapore's capital stock and its GDP. In the short-term, the granger causality ran from GDP growth to increases in capital stock. The granger causality from changes in capital stock to GDP growth is statistically insignificant.

4. CAPITAL GROWTH AND TOTAL FACTOR PRODUCTIVITY GROWTH IN SINGAPORE

Under the framework of growth accounting, economic growth is attributable to increases in factor inputs and improvements in total factor productivity (TFP). Factor inputs commonly included in growth accounting exercises are physical capital, labor force and human capital, while TFP is measured as the residual of the growth equation after accounting for the increases in factor inputs. TFP would include both technological progress and enhanced efficiency, although the contributions from these two factors are not distinguishable from the derived estimates.

In almost all studies on growth accounting, such as Hall and Jones (1999) and King and Levine (1994), TFP is found to account for the bulk of cross-country growth differences, while differences in physical capital accounts for little of the international differences in output growth. Thus, the long-term growth potential of an economy is often viewed to be determined by its ability to achieve and sustain a high level of TFP growth.

Singapore experienced very rapid increase in GDP between 1960s and 1990s on the back on sharp increases in factor inputs. Studies on decomposition of Singapore's economic growth, such as Tsao (1982), Young (1992, 1995), Rao and Lee (1995), Koh *et al.* (2002) and Hsieh (2002), have all pointed to the overwhelming importance of capital accumulation in propelling the growth of Singapore, and the smaller degree of contribution made by TFP growth. In addition, some of the earlier studies, such as those by Tsao (1982) and Young (1992, 1995), concluded that Singapore's TFP growth rates were negligible. The high-level of capital growth and the corresponding very low level of TFP growth have prompted Krugman (1994) and Young (1995) to cast doubt on the sustainability of

Singapore's economic growth; Krugman even predicted that Singapore could face a "Soviet-style" growth collapse.

There are two questions concerning the issue of TPF growth and capital growth. Firstly, was Singapore's TFP growth rates as low as those computed by Tsao (1982) and Young (1992, 1995). And secondly, is high capital growth the boon or the bane of sustainable economic growth?

The first question is a technical one that requires a technical answer. Young (1995) estimates that out of the 8.7% average GDP growth rate from 1966–1990, the growth in TFP averaged only 0.2%. The very low-level of TFP growth of Singapore obtained by Young, stems from his assumptions about the factors shares in the production function. Young estimates the output elasticity of capital of Singapore to be around 0.5, substantially higher than 0.35 in a typical economy (Eggertsson, 2004). Eggertsson cites the estimates of factor shares computed by Bosworth and Collins (2003) and Sarel (1997), and reasons that $\alpha = 0.35$ is more appropriate. Using the assumption of $\alpha = 0.35$, Eggertsson (2004) shows that Singapore's average TFP growth over the period 1960–2003 was at 1.4%. Eggertsson's decomposition of the economic growth of Singapore is reproduced in Table 2. In addition, Eggertsson also shows that Singapore's TFP growth rates are comparable to, if not higher than, those of the other advanced and emerging economies (see Table 3). Other studies on decomposition of growth of Singapore have also reported higher levels of TFP growth than those reported by Young. The reported TFP growth by

Table 2: Sources of growth in Singapore (1960–2003)

	1960–70	1970–80	1980–90	1990–03	1960–03
Output	9.4	8.6	7.2	6.2	7.7
Physical Capital	5.6 (60%)	4.8 (56%)	3.2 (44%)	2.6 (42%)	4.0 (52%)
Labor	1.9 (20%)	2.8 (33%)	2.2 (31%)	1.2 (19%)	2.0 (26%)
Education	0.5 (5%)	0.1 (1%)	0.3 (4%)	0.8 (13%)	0.5 (6%)
TFP	1.4 (15%)	0.9 (10%)	1.6 (22%)	1.6 (26%)	1.4 (18%)

Source: Eggertsson (2004) and author's own computation.

Note: Figures in parenthesis refer to percentage contribution to output.

Table 3: International comparison of sources of growth (1960–2000)

	Singapore	East Asia[3] (excluding China)	United States	Industrial Countries[4]
Output	7.7	6.7	3.4	3.5
Physical Capital	4.0 (52%)	3.3 (49%)	1.0 (29%)	1.4 (40%)
Labor	2.0 (26%)	1.8 (27%)	1.1 (32%)	0.8 (23%)
Education	0.5 (6%)	0.5 (7%)	0.3 (9%)	0.3 (9%)
TFP	1.4 (18%)	1.0 (15%)	0.9 (26%)	1.0 (29%)

Source: Eggertsson (2004) and writer's own computation.

Note 1: Data on Singapore is for the period 1960–2003.

Note 2: Figures in parenthesis refer to percentage contribution to output.

Wu and Thia (2002) for 1990–2000 is 1.6 percent. Hsieh (2002) estimates TFP growth for the East Asian economies using the dual approach and finds that Singapore's TFP growth to be around 1.6 to 1.9 percent between 1968 and 1990.

On the question of whether high capital growth is a boon or a bane of sustainable economic growth, the answer is less quantifiable but it is more intuitive. It can be seen from Table 2 that Singapore's growth since 1960 has been largely driven by capital accumulation; contribution from physical capital accounted for more than 50% of Singapore's output growth from 1960–2003. It is indisputable that the high rate of capital growth has contributed positively to the high economic growth rates and the rapid improvement in the living standards in Singapore. As pointed out by Ghesquiere (2006), "... notwithstanding the neo-classical concern about diminishing returns, high fixed capital formation can ensure high-growth and rising living standards from low initial levels. The transition to the "steady state" when these forces become impotent can take several decades".

[3] The 7 East Asian countries are Indonesia, Korea, Malaysia, the Philippines, Singapore, Taiwan, and Thailand.

[4] The 22 industrial countries are Australia, Austria, Belgium, Canada, Denmark, Finland, France, Germany, Greece, Iceland, Ireland Italy, Japan, Netherlands, New Zealand, Norway, Portugal, Spain, Sweden, Switzerland, United Kingdom, and the United States.

Furthermore, the high rate of capital accumulation has built a strong physical foundation for Singapore that serves as a platform for future growth. It can be seen from Table 2 that the early strong contributions of physical capital and labor input have eased over time falling from 60% in 1960s to 42% during 1990–2003, while TPF growth and contribution of human capital have gradually increased.

CONCLUSION

The case study of Singapore shows that as Singapore underwent transformation from a developing economy to an industrializing economy, Singapore experienced rapid capital growth. Capital growth slows down as Singapore transforms into a developed economy. These results concur with the hypothesis of the S-Curve of capital accumulation. In addition, the rapid development of Singapore was accompanied by a rising ACOR. This rising ACOR is part and parcel of the development process and does not necessarily mean that Singapore is inefficient in utilizing its capital. Singapore's ACOR is expected to eventually stabilize or even decline.

Empirical exercise shows that the long-term causal relationship between Singapore's capital stock and GDP is found to be positive and bi-directional. In the short-term, GDP growth granger caused increases in capital stock. This chapter reasons that in the case of Singapore, strong growth in physical capital during the earlier stage of our development is necessary to fuel past, present and future economic growth. In addition, a high-level of capital stock is likely to serve as the foundation for future gains in TFP. Study has shown that as Singapore's economy matures, contribution from physical capital diminishes while contributions from TFP and human capital increase.

END NOTES

Blomstrom, M, RE Lipsey and M Zejan (1996). Is fixed investment the key to economic growth? *Quarterly Journal of Economics,* 111(1), pp. 269–276.

Bosworth, BP and SM Collins (2003). The empirics of growth: An update. *Brookings Papers on Economic Activity,* 2003(2), pp. 113-206.

De Long, JB and LH Summers (1991). Equipment investment and economic growth. *Quarterly Journal of Economics,* 106(2), pp. 445-502.

De Long, JB and LH Summers (1993). How strongly do developing economies benefit from equipment investment? *Journal of Monetary Economics,* 32(3), pp. 395-415.

Department of Statistics (1997). *Multifactor Productivity Growth in Singapore: Concept, Methodology and Trends.* Department of Statistics, Singapore.

Eggertsson, G (2004). Medium-Term Growth Prospects. In *Singapore: Selected Issues.* Washington: International Monetary Fund.

Ghali, KH and A Al-Mutawa (1999). The intertemporal causal dynamics between fixed capital formation and economic growth in the group-of-seven countries. *International Economic Journal,* 13(2), pp. 31-37.

Ghesquiere, H (2006). *Singapore's Success: Engineering Economic Growth.* Singapore: Thomson Learning Asia.

Hall, RE and CI Jones (1999). Why do some countries produce so much more output per worker than others? *Quarterly Journal of Economics,* 114(1), pp. 83-116.

Hatemi-J, A and M Irandoust (2002). Investigating causal relations between fixed investment and economic growth. *Economia Internazionale/ International Economics,* 55(1), pp. 25-35.

Hsieh, CT (2002). What explains the industrial revolution in East Asia? Evidence from factor markets. *American Economic Review,* 92(3), pp. 502-526.

King, R and R Levine (1994). Capital Fundamentalism, Economic Development, and Economic Growth. *Carnegie-Rochester Conference Series on Public Policy,* 40, pp. 259-292.

Koh, SW, S Rahman and GKR Tan (2002). Growth and productivity in Singapore manufacturing industries: 1975-1998. *Asian Economic Journal,* 16(3), pp. 247-266.

Krugman, P (1994). The myth of Asia's miracle. *Foreign Affairs,* 73, pp. 62-78.

Lim, CY (1996). The trinity growth theory: The ascendancy of Asia and the decline of the West. *Accounting and Business Review,* 3(2), pp. 175-199.

Lim, CY (2004). *Southeast Asia: The Long Road Ahead,* 2nd ed. Singapore: World Scientific.

OECD (2001). *Measuring Capital: A Manual on the Measurement of Capital Stocks, Consumption of Fixed Capital and Capital Services*. Paris: OECD.

Podrecca, E and G Carmeci (2001). Fixed investment and economic growth: New results of causality. *Applied Economics,* 33(2), pp. 177–182.

Rao, B and C Lee (1995). Sources of growth in the Singapore economy and its manufacturing and service sectors. *Singapore Economic Review,* 40(1), pp. 83–115.

Sarel, M (1997). Growth and productivity in ASEAN countries, *IMF Working Paper No. 97/97*. Washington, DC: International Monetary Fund.

Sng, HY (2007). *Economic Growth and Transition: Econometric Analysis of Lim's S-Curve Hypothesis.* Unpublished PhD Thesis, Singapore: Nanyang Technological University.

Tsao, Y (1982). *Growth and Productivity in Singapore: A Supply Side Analysis.* Unpublished PhD Thesis, Harvard University.

Wu, F and JP Thia (2002). Total Factor Productivity with Singaporean Characteristics: Adjusting for Impact of Housing Investment and Foreign Workers. In *Economic Survey of Singapore*. Singapore: Ministry of Trade and Industry.

Young, A (1992). A Tale of Two Cities: Factor Accumulation and Technical Change in Hong Kong and Singapore. In *NBER Macroeconomics Annual 1992*, Blanchard, OJ and S Fischer (eds.), Cambridge, MA: MIT Press.

Young, A (1995). The tyranny of numbers: Confronting the statistical realities of the East Asian growth experience. *Quarterly Journal of Economics,* 110, pp. 641–680.

Part II

Singapore and the Region in a Globalized World

Chapter

6

The Asian Financial Crisis and the Sub-Prime Mortgage Crisis: A Dissenting View*

Lim Chong Yah†

CAPITAL CONTROL AND ASIAN CRISIS

Ten years have passed since the 1997/98 Asian financial crisis hit many countries in East Asia. There has been voluminous literature on the subject on the course and causes of the crisis. Most, if not all the literature, have not covered or have avoided answering the important question of why Asian countries that had capital control did not have such a crisis, or experienced the serious contagion effect of such a crisis. Such countries included those with a diversity of

* Lecture given at the NTU-MOE Seminar 2008 at MOE on 10th March 2008. Part I of this lecture is based on a keynote speech presented at the Asian Business Case Competition @ Nanyang 2007 Roundtable Lunch at the Nanyang Executive Center, Nanyang Technological University in October 2007. Part II is on the current Sub-Prime Mortgage Crisis.

† The views expressed herein are his personal views.

balance of payments background such as China, Vietnam, India and even very much weaker economies of Myanmar, Laos, and Cambodia (Lim, 2007).

Deepening Crisis Economies

The hard-working researchers concentrated mainly on the badly-hit crisis economies of Thailand, Malaysia, Indonesia and South Korea. Some did not even bother to mention that, such market-oriented exposed economies like Hong Kong, Singapore and Taiwan also experienced serious contagion effects but had succeeded in overcoming them. The quartet of Thailand, Indonesia, South Korea and Malaysia, however, succumbed badly to the crisis. Actually, when Malaysia decided to re-introduce capital control in September 1998, the crisis in Malaysia was effectively checked. The exchange rate was maintained at US$1 to 3.8 Malaysian ringgit until de-control was re-introduced some years later.

IMF and Crisis Management

Indeed, the other prolonged crisis trio of Thailand, Indonesia and South Korea had one anti-crisis option in common. They all sought IMF help in stabilizing their exchange rates. Later statistics show that, with IMF supervising, or under IMF tutelage, their exchange rates deteriorated further (Lim, 2004). In the case of Indonesia, the exchange rates fell even much further, almost a bottomless fall. Obviously, the IMF prescription did not cure the 3 Asian patients but prolonged their agony and misery, particularly in the case of Thailand and Indonesia. The IMF's ability-to-cure reputation has been seriously dented up to this day.

Of interest is that, not long before the crisis, the World Bank had come out with a report heralding Thailand, Malaysia and Indonesia as among the miracle economies of Asia (World Bank, 1993). Till today, however, ten years later, unfortunately for the world, particularly the developing world, the IMF still has neither changed its conventional chest of medical cures, nor its basic *modus operandi* to save the world from a foreign exchange rate crisis, as has been its avowed primary function.

Accumulate, Accumulate, Accumulate

The fall in the confidence level in IMF must have contributed importantly to the new economic phenomenon in Asia: "each unto itself" policy. Each country to accumulate as much foreign exchange reserves as possible as a precautionary measure in case another exchange rate crisis were to break out. All Asian countries have learned not to depend on the IMF for crisis salvation. Why they are all still members of the IMF is an interesting question. There must be very good reasons, mainly non-economic, on balance, not to get out of the pack. Only Venezuela has left the IMF.

Recurrence of Crisis

Ten years have passed. Can another East Asian exchange rate crisis recur? This is an interesting, important and a frequently asked question, especially before the current sub-prime crisis broke out. In my view, it will not recur in the foreseeable future, for the following 4 reasons:

(1) Unlike the 1997/98 crisis years, all the affected Asian nations now have good and respectable balance of payment surpluses. The badly affected nations then all suffered from, to use an expression in the IMF charter, "fundamental disequilibrium in the balance of payments" (Lim, 2004).
(2) The Asian nations have accumulated much more foreign exchange reserves than ever before. Their accumulate, accumulate and accumulate policy has succeeded. Most of them now have money to lend to the USA. Indeed, in the present sub-prime crises are affecting many world-class banking and financial institutions, the Singapore Government agencies: the Government of Singapore Investment Corporation Pte Ltd. (GIC) and Temasek Holdings (Private) Limited, acting in their own economic and commercial interests, have made available billions of dollars ($22 billion) to

help out blue-chip iconic financial institutions like UBS, Citigroup and Merril Lynch.

(3) The Asian nations except Hong Kong and some Gulf States, have all adopted a floating exchange rate regime, providing a cushioning affect on exchange rate movement. The degree of floating, including the basket of currencies and the floating band, however, varies from country to country.

(4) Their regulatory authorities now have more experience in regulating the banking and exchange rate system than before. They have all learned to pay more respect to the "Impossible Trinity" in their monetary and exchange rate management, the later formulated "Chiang Mai Initiative" swap arrangement notewithstanding.

The Impossible Trinity

What is this "Impossible Trinity"? The text-book Impossible Trinity Theory sets out three objectives. It maintains that not all the three objectives can be achieved simultaneously. There is "trilemma" in the three objectives. One objective is exchange rate pegging. The second objective is an independent monetary policy. The third objective is no control on capital account.

Before the 1997 crisis, Thailand pursued all the three objectives simultaneously, explaining the eruption of the crisis in Thailand in 1997. Malaysia later successfully stopped the contagion crisis with the re-introduction of capital control, i.e., effectively removing itself from the third objective. Indonesia and Thailand also removed the pegging objective, but with inappropriate measures pursued by the IMF, the crisis in both countries was prolonged and aggravated (Lim, 2004). There were, *inter alia*, runs on their banks.

The ASEAN Lost Decade

The fact that the Southeast Asian nations are now better prepared for an exchange rate crisis does not necessarily imply that their economies are now much more robust from all perspectives. Up to the time of writing in October, 2007, none of the original ASEAN 5 economies, including Singapore, have regained their pre-crisis exchange rate parity. The Indonesian rupiah, e.g., at 9,143 rupiahs to US$1 is still 275% lower than the pre-crisis rate of 2,433 rupiahs. Thailand's bahts at 31.55 bahts to a US dollar is still 27.73% lower than the pre-crisis level of 24.70 bahts to US$1. The Philippines, perennially under IMF tutelage, before and during the crisis, is worst than Thailand: the Peso has fallen by 69.42%. Only the Singapore dollar has rebounded quite close to the pre-crisis level. The Singapore government rightly used the National Wages Council (NWC), not the IMF, to fight the crisis (Lim, 2008).

Even the 2004 per capita GDPs show that, all the original ASEAN 6 contries, including Singapore, still had lower per capita income in US dollar terms than what they had, before the crisis. Thailand showed the worst result, with still a 17% decrease in per capita GDP between 1996–2004. Can we say that the crisis impact was the loss of 8 to 10 years for ASEAN in real GDP growth? Not really. Vietnam, with capital control, increased its corresponding real per capita GDP growth by 68%. Even the much criticized Myanmar, also with capital control, had a corresponding real per capita GDP increase by 47%.[1] Thus, can we say, with some qualifications, that the crisis ushered in a decade of lost years for the original ASEAN 6, but not for the new ASEAN 4? This may be said with some justification (Lim, 2007).

However, the recent US sub-prime crisis has ushered in another important dimension to the recovery of the Southeast Asian economy. The recent fall in the US dollar and its impact on the Southeast Asian exchange rates and GDP in US dollar terms have to be taken into consideration. The US dollar's depreciation in itself will lift up the Southeast Asian GDP in US dollar terms, but the direct and indirect transmission of the recession from the USA is likely to somewhat lower the real GDP growth rates in Southeast Asia.

Capital Control, Trade, GDP and FDI

Returning to the subject of the 1997/98 crisis, it should be mentioned that Malaysia has still not made its currency fully convertible, which

[1] Vietnam and Myanmar, 2005 figures.

incidentally, is still the position taken by China, Vietnam or India today and during the crisis period. One question which must be asked is that, with some control on the capital account, countries like China, Vietnam and India have displayed superlative growth rates and for relatively long periods. Why is it then necessary to abolish all capital controls in all its manifestations as advocated by the IMF and the so called Washington Consensus? A related question is: why was it that, notwithstanding the pursuit of stringent capital control in a preceding period, Japan, South Korea and Taiwan could also witness superlative growth rates for long periods? Obviously, capital control had no effect on their trade expansion, FDI inflow or the GDP growth of so many Asian dynamic economies (Lim, 2005).

Meaning of Capital Control

One must add that capital control is likely to mean there is no control over the flow of funds for trade: visible and invisible trade, income transfers and FDI flows. The restriction, in varying degrees, is on large-scale, short-term, purely speculative capital inflow and outflow of the hedge fund type. Even such a capital control can be made nominal in character in normal times.

Genesis of New Crisis

However, it would be wrong to assume that an Asian financial crisis will originate from a country in Asia. The crisis may not be homegrown. It could be imported or transmitted. All the 4 economic crises in Singapore: in 1973–1974, 1985, 1998 and 2001–2003, since Independence, were transmitted from outside. The current sub-prime crisis originates from the USA. The Northern Rock, one British bank, had a bank run. Queues of people wanted to withdraw their deposits. Britain never had a bank run in 100 years.[2]

---

[2] Several days before Easter in March 2008, there was a run by US financial institutions on a world-renowned US investment bank (Bear Stearns), resulting in the reported sale of the bank to JP Morgan Chase, for a fraction of its original worth.

THE SUB-PRIME CRISIS

About ten years ago, the sub-prime mortgage crisis began to surface in the United States. The loans to borrowers to buy a house were sub-prime because the borrowers had no collateral to offer, except the agreed-to-purchase house as a mortgage. As long as house prices kept rising, the question of re-payment or servicing the loan was not a problem to the lenders. The value of the house used as a collateral would exceed, in most cases far exceed, the loans lent out. The process went on and on and the sub-prime mortgage practice expanded by leaps and bounds, ushering further buoyancy in the housing sector and the economy as a whole. The housing boom was sustained and appeared sustainable. Everyone, including the transactions regulators, not just the ubiquitous mortgagers and the numerous mortgagees, was happy. The mortgages could also be marketed in bundles to finance institutions outside the USA, principally to Western Europe.

The serious problem came, when the housing bubble burst. When house prices took a nose-drive, borrowers' loans began to exceed the values of the mortgaged houses. The borrowers, being sub-prime, had little or no money to pay back to the banks or other lending financial intermediaries. The problem led to more serious problems, aggravating with time as more and more borrowers started to loose their mortgages. Foreclosures became rampant. More and more financial institutions got involved. There was the increasing fear that the bubble burst would lead the US into a recession with consequent recessionary impact on the global economy.

For the US economy, the sub-prime housing mortgage problem was aggravated by fossil oil price increases and the dead-weight war expenditure in Iraq. US in recent years, under the free-spending practice encouraged by the State, began to encounter more and more serious balance of trade deficit on oil account as well as on the overall trade account. The country's overspending policy, though raising the standards of living all round in good times, has resulted in the persistent balance of payment crisis on current account. The US began to have a balance of payment on current account deficit with almost every economy on earth, not just with China but also with Japan, South Korea, Taiwan, Hong Kong, the oil-exporting Middle East, the European Union, Canada and Mexico, although the imbalance with China was the most serious and caught most of the attention by the US leadership. The fear that this general imbalance would lead to a depreciation of the US dollar did occur, the moment the Federal Reserve interest rate was lowered in August 2007 as a pre-emptive move to avert a recession originating from the sub-prime crisis.

Fear of a recession in the US increased with time. This fear spread to the rest of the world, with all the stock-markets becoming the first victims. Share prices everywhere from New York to Tokyo, Hong Kong, Singapore to London, Frankfort and Paris all began to plummet. Fear fed on fear in a circular cumulative causation process across countries and within each country.

The Federal Reserve under Dr Ben Bernanke started to cut interest rate, but in a little-by-little fashion. Between 12 August 2007 and 11 December 2007, the rate was cut 4 times, either by 0.25% point or by 0.50% point. This little-by-little piece-meal method was ineffective in averting the crisis. The sub-prime generated storm became more and more serious. Finally, the Federal Reserve used a shock therapy, by suddenly cutting interest rate further by 0.75% point. This, plus the final announcement of a fiscal stimulus package by the Government had a reassuring impact on investors. The stock-market all over went on forward gear, rebounded somewhat. Could the crisis be averted?[3]

The Liquidity Trap

Of note is that initial interest rate cuts alone could not have done the trick. In my view, it would most likely lead to a liquidity trap. More money supply does not guarantee that more money would be demanded. The marginal efficiency of capital has to be raised before more demand for money could take place. The problem had to be handled both from the supply side and the demand side. Besides, if

[3] No. The mortgage crisis became more serious. A few days ago before Easter, another 0.75% point cut was announced.

one is told of a further cut in a short while, one tends to procrastinate or postpone borrowing.

Indeed, when the Japanese housing bubble burst in the late 1980s, the interest rate was eventually cut to near zero percent. This did not revive the economy. The marginal efficiency of capital declined with each interest rate cut. The Japanese economic slowdown persisted up to this day.

The housing bubble bursts in Japan and in the US have one more attribute in common. Both Governments run a serious budget deficit in good times. When the lean years appear, further deficits might result in more taxation at the wrong time. If the further deficits were financed by printing of more money, inflation would result. And Dr Bernanke is most fearful of any inflation. More taxes, however, would make the recession worse. The policy-makers hoped that more expenditure, would be financed by both local and foreign borrowing. This increased expenditure would hopefully put the incipient recession to an end. The question of paying back the increased debts would be left to the next President to solve, not the current incumbent, Mr George Bush.

If the US had a budget surplus and had accumulated reserves, the solution would be much simpler; utilize the accumulated reserves to finance the new deficit. But the US had twin deficits, serious ones at that, for quite some-time already. That was the Bush Administration's mismanagement of the economy. Indeed, the profligate policy of the US Treasury does not even qualify USA for joining the European Union. This is because of the latter's much more stringent standard in budgetary deficit policy, of not exceeding 3% of the GDP in the worst of times, and a fiscal balance in normal times.

Besides, the central bank in the US appears most reluctant to act as a lender of last resort, which is one of its basic functions. It does not want to bail out the financial institutions in trouble. It could not overcome the moral hazard problem. Some well-known iconic institutions like Citigroup, Merrill Lynch and Morgan Stanley, thus, sought a helping line from outside, like from the Sovereign Wealth Funds, such as Temasek Holdings (Private) Limited and the Government of Singapore Investment Corporation Pte Ltd (GIC). If the economic conditions deteriorate further within and outside the USA, the help of other Sovereign Wealth Funds such as from China's CIC and from the Gulf States might have to be resorted to. Japan, which has the second largest foreign exchange reserves in the world, appeared quite reticent on this matter, except that Japan has declared that it would neither lower any interest rate nor have a fiscal stimulus. In parenthesis, one could add that Japan had this experience of fighting a recession and slow growth earlier, before the US sub-prime crisis.

The Unanswered Questions

Three basic issues in this sub-prime generated turmoil have remained unanswered:

(1) The role of the regulator not just as a lender of last resort but as a preventor of first resort. Why did the US central bank allow the sub-prime problem to emerge and to become so serious, including the world-wide contagion effect? Should Mr Alan Greenspan, the famous financial wizard not shoulder some responsibility in the spread and multiplication of the sub-prime mortgages in the USA under his nose as the Chairman of the US central bank?

(2) Why did Dr Bernanke, the present Chairman, not have shock therapy to begin with, and to have the support of an effective fiscal package to handle the sub-prime crisis?[4] Could it be that the Federal Reserve and the US Treasury were not certain about the impending recession or stagflation? At times, the US central bank appeared to be more worried about inflation than recession. This uncertainty and ambiguity in the diagnosis must have contributed to the type of extremely mild and seemingly uncoordinated prescriptions.[5]

(3) The complete silence of the globally well-known Council of Economic Advisers on such a serious economic matter. What has gone wrong?

---

[4] Near Easter, the Fed cut its internal rate by a further 0.75%, another of its piece-meal exercise. This will again the perceived as a palliative, rather than an effective cure.

[5] No package of monetary and fiscal measures have been announced thus far.

The World Sovereign Wealth Funds (SWFs)

One more important point should be mentioned, the rightness of the Asian nations in accumulating foreign exchange reserves to meet the needs of a possible financial crisis, whether it originates from a balance of payment problem or from other sources are quite immaterial. The prescription for the malady is there and is available. Another point worth mentioning is that the IMF remains quite reticent throughout on the US crisis particularly on sermons on its causes and cures. Is it because the IMF has no effective role to play when the US Treasury is involved? Or is it because the US economy is too big for the IMF to handle or help? Probably, both factors are relevant to the IMF option in non-involvement or advice given to the US Treasury or the Federal Reserve Board or the managers of the SWFs to assist in limiting the sub-prime crisis from metastasizing within and beyond the USA.

Economic Theory and Economic Management

Three economic theories that are particularly relevant to the search for a solution to the prevailing sub-prime mortgage crisis in the USA will be briefly discussed here. (1) Monetarism, (2) Keynesianism and (3) the S curve hypothesis.

(1) *Monetarism*

Monetarism postulates the control of money supply to regulate inflation. The greatest advocate of this approach was Milton Friedman. He had a point. He argued that inflation is a monetary phenomenon. One should thus reduce money supply to fight inflation. In his time particularly in the late 1960s and early 1970s, the huge US budget deficit was financed by the printing of more money. Thus, the cure must be to cut down money supply. The text-book inflation equation $\pi = \dot{m} - \dot{y} + \dot{v}$ (Lim, 2004) has general validity, where π refers to the inflation rate, $\dot{m}$— growth rate of money supply, $\dot{y}$— real GDP growth rate and $\dot{v}$— the change in the velocity of circulation of money. If the diagnosis is inflation, as appeared to be the position taken by the European Central Bank, then a monetarist solution is particularly relevant. This may include the upping of interest rate.

However, in the US sub-prime crisis, inflation is not, or not yet, the problem. The problem is recession. The European Central Bank, however, did not share this view. It was afraid of inflation in Europe. As stated earlier, this equivocation arose from the equivocal diagnosis of the sub-prime crisis. Even in the USA, the severity was underestimated. This probably accounted for the miniscule cut in the interest rate and up to the time of writing 5 separate cuts had to be made and in such a short span of time. But Friedman was handling inflation, not recession.

(2) *Keynesianism*

More relevant to handling a recession is Keynesianism. In Keynes's General Theory, only recession was featured. To Keynes, in a recession, monetary policy alone would not be effective. In other words, cheap monetary policy alone would not work. The reason is that it does not automatically lead to an increase in effective demand. Then firstly, why did Dr Bernanke use interest rate to fight the impending recession? Secondly, why did he commence the fight in a crawling, bit-by-bit, process? Probably, he has no influence over the US Treasury and its fiscal policy. Besides, he probably also underestimates the seriousness of the mortgage crisis. Thirdly, he probably was not aware that Japan in earlier years failed to lift up its economy by cutting interest rate even to near zero percent.

Ultimately, in the US, fiscal policy had to be roped in, as is the main advocacy of Keynesianism. To Keynes, to fight a recession, one must run a budget deficit. One must increase public spending: more spending, more spending and more spending.

But it was during the US presidential primaries that Senator Hillary Clinton, one of the most-prominent candidates, advocated a US$70 billion injection into the fiscal system. Senator Barack Obama, her equally prominent rival in the Democratic front, maintained that

US$70 billion was insufficient. It should be US$80 billion.The outcome of the debate is that Mr George Bush, the Republican President, proposed a US$150 billion fiscal stimulus, simply by adding the two proposals! The President's proposal has been eventually accepted by the US Congress. But US$150 billion may sound so big to the outside world. It is, however, only a trifle for by far the biggest economy in the world. It adds up to only 1% of US GDP! Can this be an effective counter-recession policy? I doubt the adequacy and therefore the effectiveness. But if the world believes in this cure, it could still work. US thus would not slip into a technical recession, defined as two consecutive negative real growth rates on a q-o-q (quarter on quarter) basis.

The 1998 Crisis in Singapore

When Singapore was faced with the Asian financial crisis in 1998, the deflation in money income and costs of production advocated and adopted by the Singapore Government came to 20% of our GDP. One third took the form of cuts in taxes and fees. One third was a cut in employers' contribution to CPF and the other third was a cut in end-of the year bonuses (Lim, 1998). True, Singapore could get from accumulated reserves, if it wanted to. Since the US made no contingency reserve provision, the financing might have to come from more foreign borrowing and if need be, from the printing of more money. Recession in the post-Keynesian world can be quite easily handled, particularly if preparedness is there. That preparedness does not appear to be there in the USA.There has also been excessive reliance on monetary policy, side-lining the increase in effective demand option.

The US Twin Deficits

The US twin deficits would be worsened, with the US budget stimulus.The bigger the budget stimulus, the bigger will be the US budget and current account deficits.The bigger current account deficit could easily generate bigger pressures for the further depreciation of the US dollar. The East Asian nations are now facing a different foreign exchange adjustment problem. In the 1997/98 crisis, the US dollar appreciation left many of those countries having to devalue. Now, it is the opposite. But the pressure on foreign exchange adjustment is easier to handle in an appreciating local currency than to follow the US dollar's upward movement. In the former case, they can just sell more of their local money. In the later case, they need more foreign reserves to buy up more local currencies.

(3) *The S Curve Hypothesis*

According to this hypothesis, the developed economies, being already well developed, will display a low rate of GDP growth, from 1% to 4%, when the built-in growth momentum is to be depended upon, for further growth. A higher growth rate (>4%) has to come from seismic changes in the growth parameters. The theory also postulates that, growth is to come from more capital spending, the expansion of productive capacity; effective production. This means production to meet market demand, including foreign demand. Zero or negative savings rate in the US can only lead to balance of payments problem. It also implies poor performance by a large number of corporations with little undistributed profits (savings) for expansion or into new lines of corporate endeavors.

The US stimulus package, though small, relative to the US economy, is focussed on consumption spending, not on capital expenditure. This is likely to result in more serious current account deficit, which means greater pressure for the US dollar to depreciate and more pressure for China to re-value.

This balance of payments pressure did not happen to Japan. This is because Japan had and still has only the budget deficit problem to contend with. It had and still has huge current account surpluses. Besides, Japan did not have to depend upon foreign countries to buy its treasury bills to finance its budget deficit. It is through internal borrowing. Notwithstanding that, the repayment burden of the society through taxes cannot be overlooked. The passing of the debt burden to future generations has become quite fashionable in some developed countries. The term used is the inter-generation transfer of debt burden. So, if the S Curve Theory is correct, if the US economy rebounds, which, with the effluxion of time, the rebounded real GDP growth rate will slow-down, to the levels of Japan and Western Europe, with, however, the twin deficit problems unresolved. The slow-down in the US will be from the hitherto 3%–4%, the upper range of the S Curve to the lower range of 1–2%, which is the characteristic of the S Curve for old matured economies of Europe and Japan.

However, if the housing mortgage crisis metastasizes into, say, a sub-prime credit card crisis, then there would be no choice for the US Treasury but to increase the budget stimulus as a rescue operation. At any rate, the US Treasury and the Federal Reserve Board would have to operate in consort with each other to effect the optimum anti-recessionary impact. They seem to operate separately and independently, up to this point, i.e., one direct attack on the sub-prime problem is, for the State to encourage the re-payment of prior mortgage rates within, say, the next 4 years, at a reducing subsidized rate of 40% to 30%, 20%, and then to 10%, with the State and the lenders (mortgagees) co-shouldering an equal share of the burden. The State pays the fine for the negligence of regulatory oversight; the mortgagees, for greed in sub-prime lending. This rescue device has to be accompanied by more and more investment, supplemented by greater FDI inflows, including WSF inflows into the open sectors. The alternative is for the economy to slide down to recession, and if only aggressive interest rate cut is used, the end-result is likely to be the continuation or even aggravation of the sub-prime malaise. Inflationary pressures, however, might willy nilly be the ultimate cure, as such pressures could result in the rise in asset prices, including house prices, as well, with the public paying the general price for a general lower standard of living. The country could blunder its way through.

END NOTES

The World Bank (1993). *The East Asian Miracle: Economic Growth and Public Policy*. New York: Oxford University Press.

NWC Secretariat, November (1998). *NWC: Memorandum to the Prime Minister, 1972–1998.*

Lim, CY (2004). *Southeast Asia: The Long Road Ahead*, (2nd Ed.), Chap. 12, The Asian Financial Crisis", Singapore: World Scientific, pp. 335–340.

Lim, CY (2005). Economic theory and the East Asian region. *The Singapore Economic Review*, Special 50th Anniversary Issue, pp. 495–512.

Lim, CY (2007). The International Monetary Fund and exchange rate management. *The Singapore Economic Review*, 52(3), Special Issue pp. 285–294.

Chapter

7

Asian Economic Integration: The Role of Singapore

Pradumna Bickram Rana

INTRODUCTION

Along with the high rates of saving and investment and high levels of education, an important component of East Asia's development model of the past five decades or so, was to open its economies to international trade and investment. This drive involved granting trade preferences to all countries unilaterally — the so-called "most-favored-nation" approach under the GATT/WTO framework. The focus was on "sequential" not "interdependent" development. Described in Akamatsu's (1962) "flying geese" analysis, the model involved the transfer of export markets from the more advanced to less advanced countries. Japan began as a producer of low-priced final consumer goods and later moved on into capital-intensive intermediate and capital goods. Then the second-generation countries (the newly industrializing economies (NIEs) comprising Hong Kong, China; Republic of Korea; Taiwan; and Singapore) moved into the vacated consumer goods assembly in the 1960s. Similarly, in the 1970s and the 1980s the third (Indonesia, Malaysia, Philippines, and Thailand) and the fourth generation countries

(People's Republic of China (PRC) and Viet Nam) moved in to fill the gaps left by the NIEs. An alternative description of the East Asian development pattern is the S Curve theory of Lim (2004). Here we have the "elephants", "horses", and "turtles" moving along the S curve.[1] In terms of economic and social transformation, East Asia achieved in 40 years what took 300 years in Europe (Mahbubani, 2008).

Despite the lack of integrationist approach in the East Asian development model, the region's market-led integration with the world flourished in tandem with its integration with the region (at least, in absolute terms) (see Fig. 1).[2] This was because of policy reforms, economic dynamism, and the establishment of vertical production networks. Since The financial crisis of 1997–1998 focused the region's attention on its inter-dependence and shared interests and East Asia became keen to support market-led integration with policy efforts.[3,4] The major factor that ignited the interest of East Asian countries to regional monetary and financial integration was the virulent contagion of the East Asian financial crisis and the policy mistakes made by the IMF in managing it.[5] It was also felt that the resources of the IMF were fairly limited and that it

[1] This approach differed from the Latin American and the African development model where import-substitution policies at the national level were expanded to cover geographical sub-regions (e.g., the Latin American Free Trade Area and the Latin American Common Market). They were "closed regionalism" and did not do well.

[2] Unless mentioned otherwise, East Asia is defined as ASEAN+3 (ASEAN plus PRC, Japan, and Republic of Korea) plus Hong Kong, China and Taipei.

[3] Economic integration refers to the elimination of frontiers to the flow of goods, services, and factors of production. It can be market-led or policy led. Market-led integration is increasing convergence of economic parameters due to activities of market participants while policy-led integration is due to national policies to enhance regional cooperation.

[4] Another paradigm shift in the East Asian model is the emphasis placed on financial sector development. For various reasons, this sector was repressed during the pre-crisis period. The Asian financial crisis also ignited the debate on the reform of the international financial architecture including the reform of the IMF.

[5] Given that the Asian financial crisis was a capital account crisis, the IMF should not have required Asian countries to tighten fiscal policy and raise interest rates. It should also not have gone overboard in requiring these countries to meet many structural conditions that were imposed in its program. Its approach to financial and corporate reforms was also inappropriate, at least, in Indonesia (Isard, 2005). Subsequently, the IMF accepted many of these criticisms (IMF, 2003).

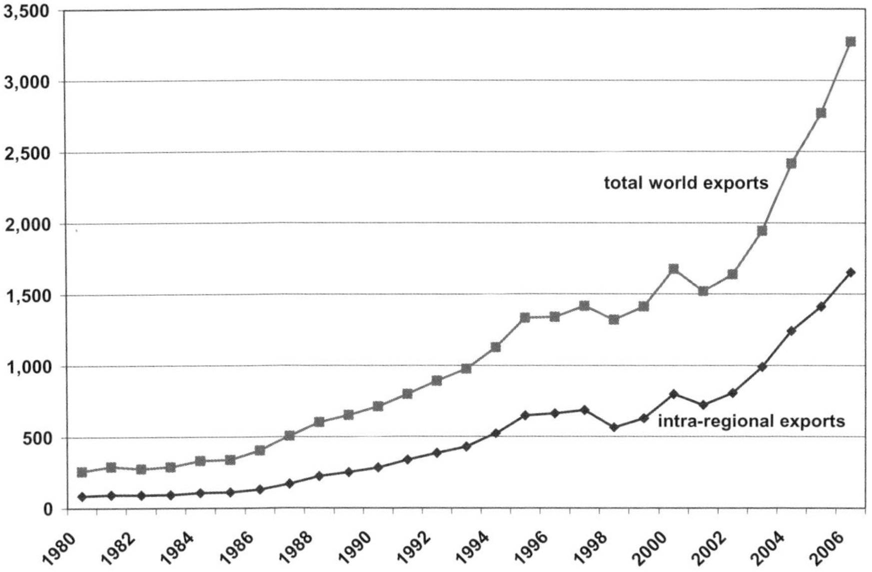

Source: IMF, Direction of Trade Statistics CD-Rom, June 2007.

Figure 1: East Asia-15: Global and regional integration (in billion USD)

might not have adequate resources to handle a capital-account crisis associated with large surges and outflows of short-term private capital. Slow progress in the Doha Round under the auspices of the World Trade Organization (WTO) and the popularity of regionalism elsewhere (e.g., European Union (EU) and North American Free Trade Agreement (NAFTA)) also encouraged East Asian countries to promote regionalism in trade (Kawai, 2005). Additional factors were the desire to internalize the benefits of growing interdependence and the realization that regionalism could help maximize the benefits of globalization and minimize the costs. In the post-crisis period, East Asia realized that it needed to be more self-reliant and gain fuller control of its destiny (MAS, 2007).

Regionalism in Asia has two features. First, it covers four areas in terms of scope — trade, finance, macroeconomic policy/monetary integration and regional public goods (e.g., environment and water sharing).[6] Second, in terms of geographical coverage, it has been

[6] This chapter does not cover issues related to the fifth pillar of regional cooperation and integration in regional public goods.

mainly bilateral or subregional. More recently, bridges are also starting to be built across the subregions (e.g., the initiation of the East Asia Summit and the large number of free trade agreements (FTAs) under negotiation between South Asia and East Asia).

Against this background, the objectives of this Chapter are to: (1) review trends in East Asian regionalism including identifying the next steps (2) review trends in the second phase of Asian economic integration which is the evolution of economic relations between South Asia and East Asia or Pan-Asian integration, and (3) discuss Singapore's role.

TRADE, FINANCE, AND MACROECONOMIC POLICY/MONETARY INTEGRATION IN EAST ASIA

On trade integration, East Asia has made encouraging progress with intra-regional trade reaching 55% of total trade in 2005[7] (up from 43% in 1990), which is higher than the level for NAFTA (46%) but lower than that for the EU (67%) (see Fig. 2). Much of this expansion has been driven by market forces especially the establishment of vertical production networks in the region. The traditional production networks were triangular where Japan and the NIEs exported parts for electrical appliances, office and telecom equipment and textiles and garments industry to the PRC and the third generation countries (Indonesia, Malaysia, Philippines, and Thailand) which in turn completed the processing and exported the final product to markets in the US and Europe. Since the mid-1990s, more sophisticated and complex production networks have emerged which involve transshipment of components — back and forth trade in parts and components across Asian countries (Gill and Kharas, 2007). With the rapid emergence of PRC, these networks are being increasingly centered in the PRC.

Given the uncertainties and risks in the multilateral trading system, the momentum for Free Trade Agreements (FTAs) has also

---

[7] In contrast, the level of intra-regional trade among the South Asian countries, although increasing since 1995, stood at only 5.6% in 2005.

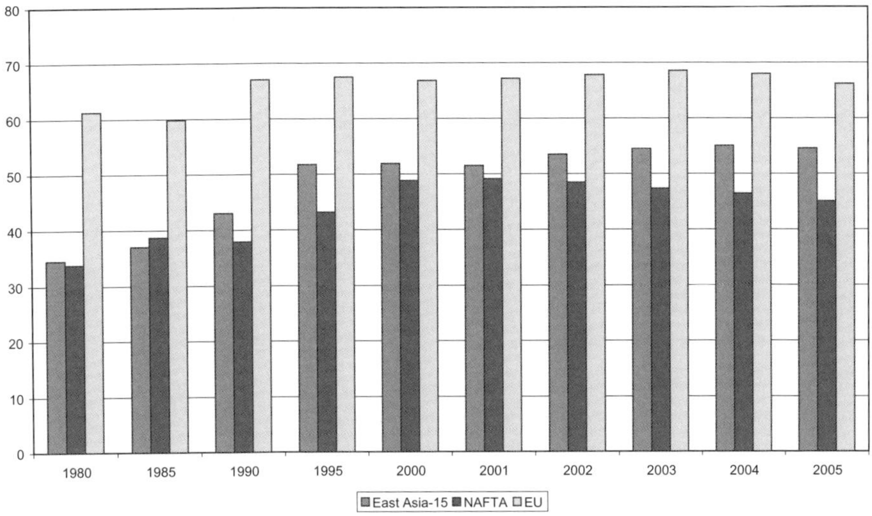

Source: IMF, Direction of Trade Statistics CD-Rom, July 2006.

Figure 2: East Asia-15 ASEAN+3, HongKong, China, and Taiwan, EU, and NAFTA Intra-regional Trade Shares (in percent)

increased in East Asia with some 175 such agreements in existence or under negotiation compared with just a handful, a decade ago. The latest are the Economic Partnership Agreements that Japan signed with Indonesia and the one it is negotiating with India (expected to be concluded by the end of next year). FTAs will no doubt proliferate further if the Doha Round continues to falter. If they are designed properly, FTAs can help countries reap the benefits of their comparative advantage. That is why FTAs are allowed as exceptions to the anti-discrimination rules of the GATT/WTO. But there is a risk that the proliferation of FTAs could come at the expense of trade with nonmembers, known as trade diversion. It could also create an "Asian noodle bowl" effect and raise administrative costs of trade. FTAs should, therefore, be consistent with WTO. They should also be compatible with other FTAs in the region. Broadening the membership of FTAs and deepening their coverage beyond tariffs into services, investments, technological cooperation, etc. (called FTA Pluses) is one way of making FTAs stepping stones rather than stumbling blocks to multilateralism.

Lack of data makes it difficult to measure the level of financial integration in East Asia, but those that are available suggest that it is now starting to increase, albeit from low levels (MAS, 2007; Rana, 2007). Available price and quantity measures of financial integration in East Asia are in Fig. 3. East Asian countries have taken collective actions to develop local currency bond markets as these markets will reduce the "double mismatch" problem, which was at the heart of the crisis, and overcome the so-called "original sin" problem.[8] The basic idea is to mobilize the region's vast pool of savings to be intermediated directly to the region's long-term investment, without going through financial intermediaries outside the region. Regional financial intermediation through bond markets would diversify the modes of

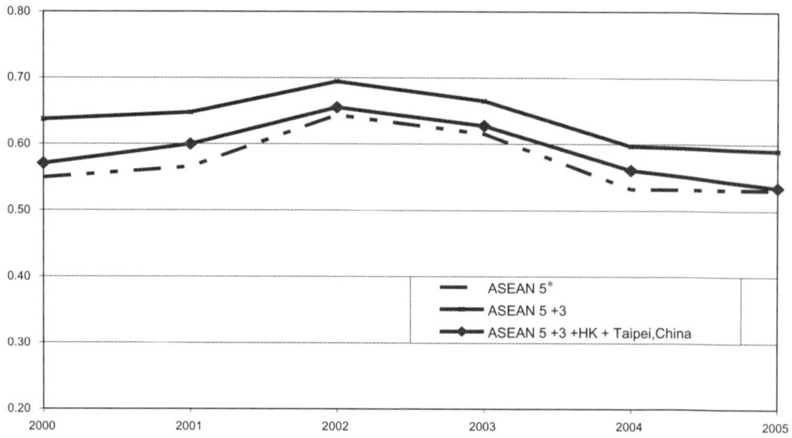

Source: Bloomberg LP.

* ASEAN 5 consists of Indonesia, Malaysia, Philippines, Singapore, and Thailand.

Figure 3(a): Coefficient of variation of prime lending market rates

---

[8] The "double mismatch" problem refers to borrowing unhedged foreign funds to lend long-term in domestic currency and borrowing short-term to lend long-term. The "original sin" is a situation where emerging economy residents cannot borrow abroad in domestic currency nor borrow long-term, even domestically. Hence domestic banks and corporations tend to face a currency or maturity mismatch or both, thus facing balance-sheet vulnerabilities to sharp changes in exchange rates and/or interest rates.

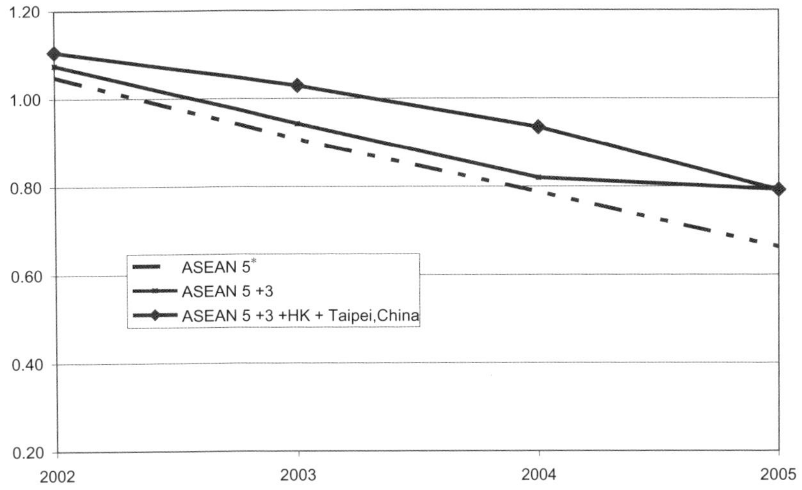

Source: Bloomberg LP.
* ASEAN 5 consists of Indonesia, Malaysia, Philippines, Singapore, and Thailand.

Figure 3(b): Coefficient of variation of money markets rates

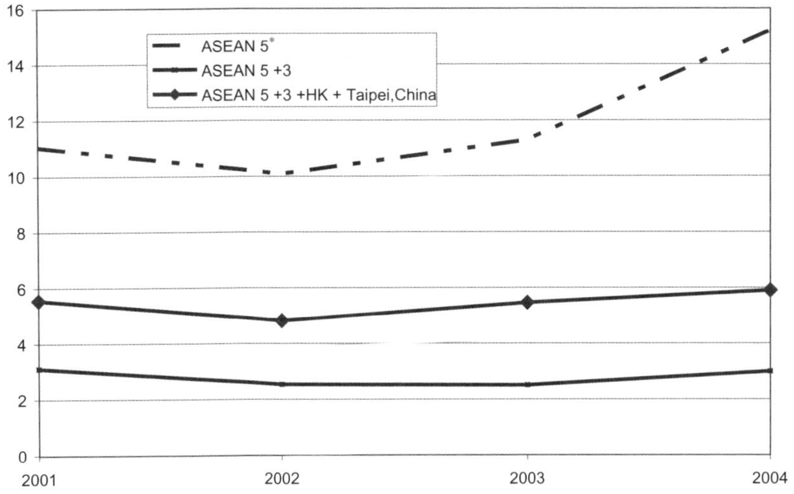

Source: International Monetary Fund, Coordinated Portfolio Investment Survey.
* ASEAN 5 consists of Indonesia, Malaysia, Philippines, Singapore, and Thailand.

Figure 3(c): Share of intra-regional portfolio investment (as % of total)

Figure 3: Financial integration in East Asia: Price and quantity indicators financing in the region and reduce the double mismatch. The initiatives include the Asia Pacific Economic Cooperation (APEC) Bond Initiative, the Executives' Meeting of East Asia Pacific central banks (EMEAP), Asian Bond Fund (ABF) Initiative and the ASEAN+3 Asian Bond Markets Initiative (ABMI).

EMEAP introduced the ABF in June 2003 in order to help expand bond markets through demand-side stimulus through central bank purchases of sovereign and quasi-sovereign bonds issued by 8 EMEAP emerging members (including PRC, Hong Kong, Indonesia, Korea, Malaysia, Philippines, Singapore, and Thailand) using all eleven members' foreign exchange reserves. The initial attempt was to purchase US$1 billion of US dollar-denominated bonds (ABF-1). Given the recognition that local-currency denominated bonds need to be promoted in order to address the "double mismatch" problem, the central bankers introduced ABF-2 in December 2004, involving purchases of US$2 billion equivalent of sovereign and quasi-sovereign local currency-denominated bonds.

Macroeconomic policy/monetary integration is essentially a post-crisis phenomenon in East Asia. There is an ascending order of intensity of these efforts in the sense that they involve progressively increasing constraints on the amount of discretion that individual countries can exercise in the design of macroeconomic policies. By level of intensity, these efforts have ranged from economic review and policy dialogue to establishing regional financing arrangements and eventually toward coordinating exchange rate policies. East Asian governments have (1) started to engage each other in policy dialogues (the two recent initiatives are the ASEAN Surveillance Process and the ASEAN+3 Economic Review and Policy Dialogue)[9]; (2) established a regional financing mechanism — the Chiang Mai Initiative (CMI) under which 16 bilateral swaps amounting to US$83 billion have been established and efforts to multilateralize the bilateral swaps

[9] The earlier initiatives under the auspices of the central banks in the region are EMEAP, SEACEN, and SEANZA. The ASEAN+3 group has also taken steps to monitor short-term capital flows and to develop early warning systems of currency and banking crises.

are ongoing; and (3) initiated discussion on how exchange policies could be coordinated possibly through the use of an Asian Currency Unit (ACU) which would be a basket of currencies. An ASEAN+3 Research Group, comprising about 30 think tanks from across the region, has been set up to support the groups.

In East Asia, most of the poor live in remote or isolated areas, especially in regions close to national borders. They need to be linked to commercial and industrial centers not only in their own countries but to those in other countries in the region and beyond — via highways, railways, ports, telecommunications, and other hard infrastructure. The "software" aspects of infrastructure development, including trade facilitation, are also important to reduce transportation costs. Greater connectivity enhances trade and investment integration by facilitating the movement of goods. The most advanced program in East Asia is the Greater Mekong Subregion — comprising Cambodia, Lao People's Democratic Republic, Myanmar, Thailand, Viet Nam, and the Yunnan Province of the PRC. Other initiatives include the Brunei Darussalam-Indonesia-Malaysia-Philippines East ASEAN Growth Area and Indonesia-Malaysia-Thailand Growth Triangle.

East Asia's market-led integration, which now, is also being driven by various policy actions, is expected to deepen further. One reason for optimism is that the increasing level of trade integration has led to a greater synchronization of output and business cycles in the region. This means that symmetric shocks are expected to prevail enhancing the case for cooperation and coordination of policies (Rana, 2008).

Going forward, Asian economic integration is expected to follow what Senior Minister Goh Chok Tong (2006) once referred to as the "variable geometry, flexible borders" approach. The process will be multi-track with a trade (including infrastructure), finance, and macroeconomic policies/monetary integration track. On the trade track, efforts should be made to (1) make the FTAs compatible with each other (by having similar rules of origin as in Europe) and (2) consolidate the proliferation of FTAs into a deeper and wider FTA such as the East Asian FTA (including India). Kawai and Wignaraja (2007) have shown that an ASEAN+6 FTA would provide more gains than an ASEAN+3 FTA. Connectivity issues including infrastructure development and trade facilitation are also being addressed.

On the finance track, Asian bond markets should be developed further. Regional institutions to deepen local-currency bond markets — such as a regional credit guarantee institution and a regional settlement agency — need to be established. With the progress in reforming market infrastructure at the national levels, a regional regulatory agency that promotes coordination of capital market rules and regulations may be developed in the future.

On the macroeconomic policy/monetary track, efforts to multilateralize the Ching Mai Initiative (CMI) should be continued. At their meeting in Hyderabad in 2006, the ASEAN+3 Finance Ministers decided that "all swap providing countries can simultaneously and promptly provide liquidity support to any parties involved in bilateral swap arrangements at times of emergency". At their Kyoto meeting in 2007, the Ministers decided to establish a "self-managed reserve pooling arrangement" for which the details are being worked out. At their May 2008 meeting in Madrid, the Ministers "agreed that the total size of the multilateralized CMI would be at least US$ 80 billion." The next steps are to further expand the size of the swaps, multilateralize it, and reduce the linkage to the IMF. Over the medium-term, a centrally administered reserve pool (a fund) could be established. As part of this process, concerted efforts must be made to establish a formal "peer review" and "peer pressure" mechanism similar to that of the OECD.

The deepening regional and financial integration in the region together with the synchronization of business cycles suggests that, East Asia should initiate actions to coordinate exchange rate policies using a step-by-step approach. The first step could be to promote greater exchange rate flexibility while maintaining a certain amount of intra-regional stability by monitoring deviations from an ACU basket (Kawai and Rana, 2008).

Some commentators see recent trends in the region as heralding the eventual adoption of a single currency or the establishment of an East Asian monetary union. Europe's experience shows that a monetary union imposes stringent demands on policy coordination and institution building that needs strong political will and a strong sense of common purpose which East Asia lacks at the present (MAS, 2007).

In addition to being multi-track, East Asian regionalism is also expected to be multi-speed — with the pace of progress for different aspects of regional cooperation and integration varying and with new members, joining as and when they feel that they are ready to do so. It will also be a bottom-up approach as compared to the European institution-led top-down approach.

Regionalism in East Asia is expected to improve the medium- and long-term economic outlook for the region and enhance the region's resilience to external shocks through the expansion of trade and investment based on comparative advantages of member countries; lead to greater monetary and financial stability and prevent financial crises; and provide cross-border connectivity which is essential for the movement of goods, services, labor, and information across countries. Competitiveness, industrial production, and productivity of East Asian countries are expected to increase.

THE SECOND PHASE OF ASIAN INTEGRATION: ECONOMIC RELATIONS BETWEEN SOUTH ASIA AND EAST ASIA[10]

Prior to 1990, South Asian and East Asian countries were relatively isolated from one another in terms of economic relations and there was little talk of Pan-Asian integration. The only trade agreement that covered the two sub-regions was the Bangkok agreement signed in 1975 (now called the Asia-Pacific trade agreement). The adoption of the "Look East Policy" in India in 1991 and similar policies in other South Asian countries together with the economic dynamism of India and PRC, has now heightened the interest in the process of Pan-Asian integration particularly on the evolving economic relationships between the two subregions.

South Asia's total merchandise trade with East Asia has grown significantly in absolute terms albeit from a low base. It increased eight-fold during 1990–2006, from US$12.4 billion to US$96.8 billion (see Fig. 4), for an average annual growth rate of 14.6%. The annual

[10] This section is based on Chapter 5 of Rana and Dowling (forthcoming 2008).

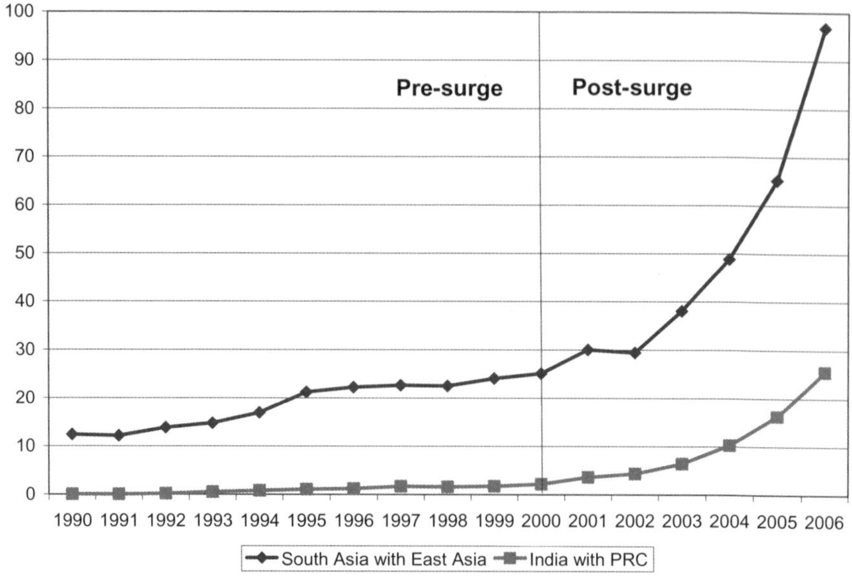

Source: IMF, Direction of Trade Statistics CD-Rom, June 2007.

Figure 4: Total trade between South Asia and East Asia (in billion dollars)

growth rate was relatively moderate until 2000, but it has surged after that, growing by 26.2% per annum. As expected, a large part of the increase in South Asia-East Asia trade is accounted by the bilateral trade between the two giant economies of India and PRC.

Data in Fig. 5 show that East Asia accounted for 18.9% of South Asia's total trade in 1990 and about 21% in 1994, before it fell back to about 18% in 2000. Since then, however, it has been increasing, reaching about 24% in 2006. On the other hand, South Asia accounted for a mere 1.3% of East Asia's trade and a slightly higher 1.9% in 2006. Hence, East Asia is a more important trading partner for South Asia than vice versa.

In 2006, Pan-Asian intra- and inter-regional trade stood at US$2.1 trillion of which East Asian intra-regional trade accounted for 93.6% followed by inter-regional trade between South Asia and East Asia (see Table 1). Intra-South Asian trade accounted for only 0.8% and intra-Central Asian trade, an even lower percentage (0.2%).

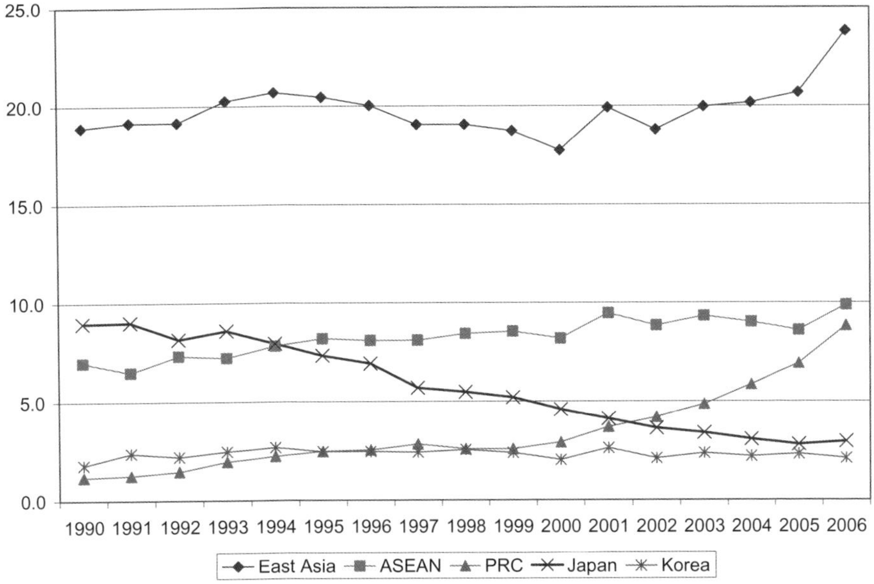

Source: IMF, Direction of Trade Statistics CD-Rom, June 2007.

Figure 5: Inter-regional trade between South Asia and East Asia (as a percentage of South Asia's total trade with the world)

Table 1: Pan-Asian and intra-regional and inter-regional trade, 2006 (in billion $)

Intra-regional Trade:	
East Asia	2,003.1 (93.6%)
South Asia	16.2 (0.8%)
Central Asia	4.3 (0.2%)
Inter-regional Trade:	
South Asia-East Asia	96.8 (4.5%)
Central Asia-South Asia	2.3 (0.1%)
Central Asia-East Asia	18.1 (0.8%)
Total Pan-Asian Trade	**2.1 trillion (100%)**

Note: Trade refers to Exports plus Imports. Figures in parentheses refer to share of Pan-Asian trade.

Source: IMF, Direction of Trade Statistics CD-Rom, June 2007.

The absence of comparable data on FDI by source limits an analysis of investment relationships between South Asia and East Asia. The data that are available from national sources and the ASEAN Secretariat show that investment relations between the two regions, although starting to increase in recent years, is still limited.

Calculation of revealed comparative advantage indices shows that, although there are overlaps there is a potential for enhancing trade between the two regions. South Asia has comparative advantage mainly in primary goods and labor-intensive manufactures and IT services, while East Asia has comparative advantage across a much wider range of products. These include primary goods such as crude rubber and fish, labor-intensive manufactures such as textiles, travel goods and footwear, and more capital- and knowledge-intensive items such as office machines and telecommunications equipments.

More recently, as in other parts of the world, there has been a proliferation of FTAs between South Asia and East Asia. The most significant of these, so far, is the signing of the India-Singapore Comprehensive Economic Cooperation Agreement (CECA) on June 2005. The CECA became effective in August 2005 and covers not only trade in goods but also services, investments and cooperation in technology, education, air services, and human resources. Various South Asian countries are also members of the Asia-Pacific Trade Agreement under the auspices of UN ESCAP. In addition, 8 FTA framework agreements have been signed between South and East Asian countries. These are the ASEAN-India, India-Thailand, BIMSTEC, PRC-Pakistan, India-Korea, Malaysia-Pakistan, Pakistan-Singapore, and Pakistan-Indonesia FTAs. Another six FTAs have been proposed — China-India, Japan-India, Malaysia-India, Pakistan-Philippines, Pakistan-Thailand, and Singapore-Sri Lanka FTAs.

A number of policy actions could be taken to increase the level of South Asia-East Asia integration. First, the levels of tariffs and NTBs are already low in many East Asian countries and since the 1990s South Asia has also made encouraging progress in the same direction. However, there is room for further reductions in tariffs and NTBs in both regions (especially NTBs in East Asia because tariffs are already low). Second, in addition to reducing tariffs and NTBs, South Asian countries and several East Asian countries also need to make progress in implementing the remaining reform agenda — namely, developing the social (e.g., schools, hospitals, rural medical centers) and physical (power, water, roads, railways) infrastructure and implementing the so-called second generation reforms to enhance transparency, good governance, and human capital.These include, among others, reforms of civil service and of delivery of public goods, creating an environment that is conducive to private sector opportunities (greater competition, better regulations, and stronger property rights), and reforms of institutions that create human capital (e.g. health and education). Third, South and East Asian countries need to consolidate their FTAs. Francois, Rana, and Wignaraja (2008 forthcoming) support this finding. Countries should also deepen FTAs — extend coverage beyond trade in goods into services, investment, technology etc.

The fourth measure that could impact significantly on the level of trade between South Asia and East Asia is the reduction of trading costs. This could be brought about through investment in trade-related infrastructure and streamlining of cross-border procedures (including customs procedures and logistic costs). Most cargo between South Asia and East Asia moves by water (see Fig. 6) and air (although South Asia does not have an air freight hub yet, Fig. 7) as there is no land transport services that are operational at the present time. Land transit through Myanmar — shown in the Asian Highway concept (Fig. 8) — is not possible at the present time.Additional corridors between India and PRC through Bhutan and Nepal will have to be developed. PRC has plans to extend the recently-opened Qinghai-Tibet railway (see Fig. 9) to Nepal and India. Regional shipping lines also have to be developed. Countries should make efforts to reduce transport and logistic constraints to facilitate movement of goods between the two regions.These include delays in customs inspection, cargo handling and transfer, and processing of documents. Customs procedures could be modernized by (1) aligning the customs code to international standards, (2) simplifying and harmonizing procedures, (3) making tariff structures consistent with the international harmonized tariff classification, and (4) adopting and implementing the WTO Customs Valuation Agreement.

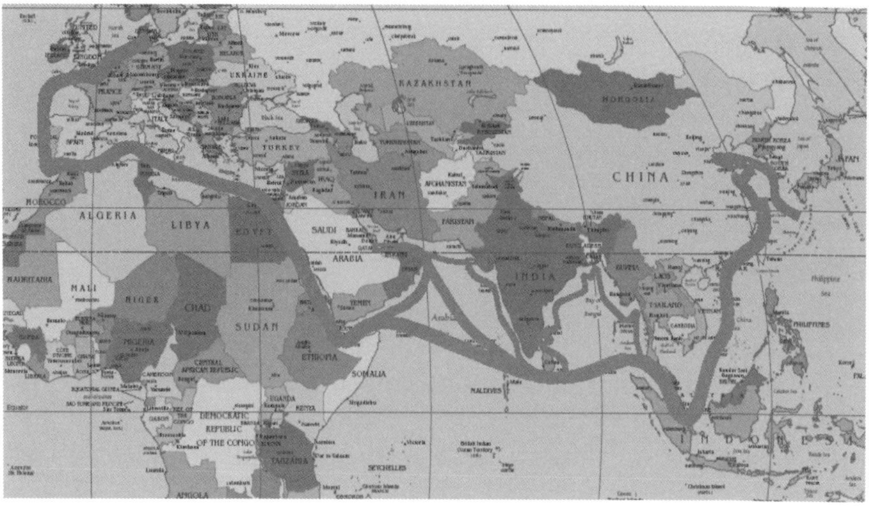

Figure 6: Infrastructure — Southern corridor: Shipping

Figure 7: Central corridor: Air freight hubs

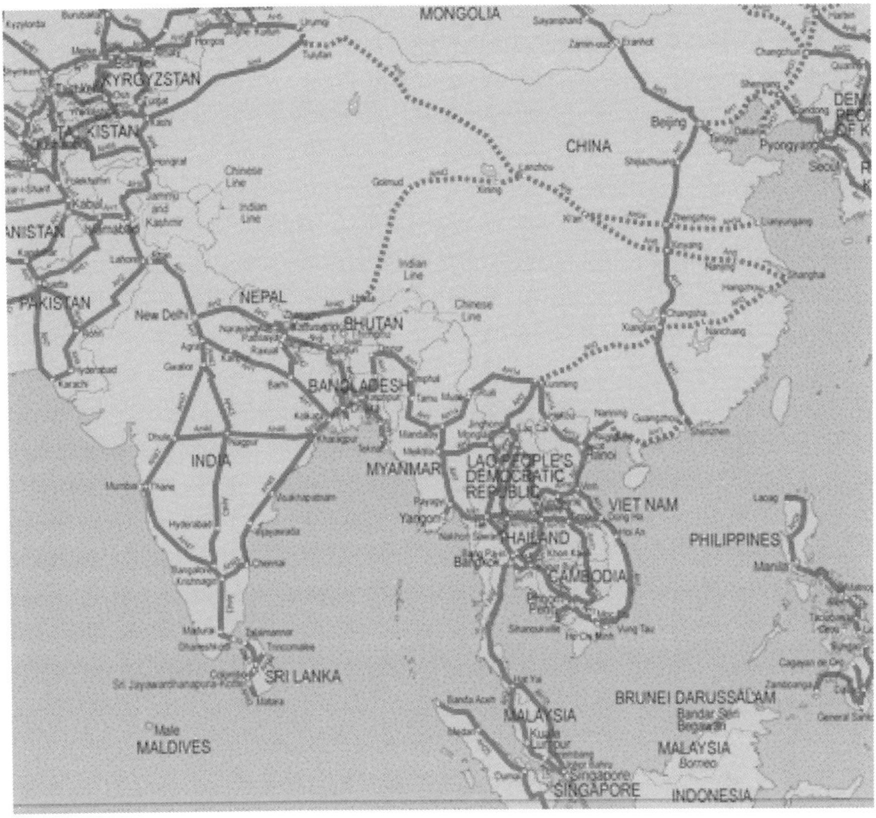

Figure 8: Northern corridor: Asian highway

Finally, trade promotion efforts through skillful economic diplomacy, regular exchange of business delegations and civil society could be encouraged a lot more. People-to-people contacts can go a long way in enhancing the level of trade and investment across countries.

THE ROLE OF SINGAPORE

Singapore is one of the most open and trade dependent country in the world and, therefore, its approach to integration is a two-track

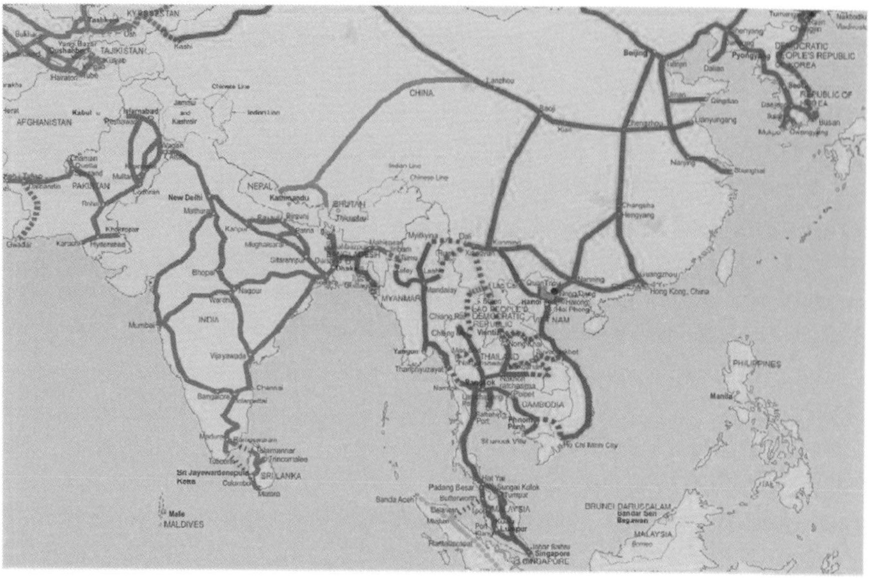

Figure 9: Northern corridor: Trans-asian railways

one. Global efforts and multilateralism is the most efficient and, therefore, the first best. However, regionalism can also be supported if it complements multilateralism. Prime Minister Lee at the APEC Summit last year said "I don't see the APEC Free Trade Agreement proposal as Plan B, I think it is complementary to the Doha Round". As a major regional and international trading and financial center, Singapore is playing an important role in Asian integration.

Singapore is involved in all sub-regional groups and it was the Chair of the APEC Summit in 2000 and the Chair of the ASEAN and East Asia Summit last year. Two important agreements were signed at the ASEAN Summit. The ASEAN Charter seeks to make integration rules based, but its ratification by members may take time. Recently, Singapore has proposed that the ASEAN minus X principle be applied so that the Charter can come into force even before each and every member has ratified it within the one-year period. The proposal to establish an ASEAN Economic Community (a single market) by 2015 is also appropriate but progress must be monitored carefully.

Singapore is active in various regional initiatives. In terms of signing FTAs, having signed 28 bilateral or plurilateral FTAs, Singapore is the most prolific among the East Asian countries. The Singapore–India Comprehensive Economic Cooperation serves as a role model for the newer generation FTAs pluses that go beyond trade into services, investment and technology cooperation. Singapore has also signed investment agreements with various countries (e.g., connectivity agreement with Viet Nam several years back and the Singapore–Viet Nam investment parks). Singapore participates actively in various regional fora chairing several working groups.

Singapore is actively involved in building links between South Asia and East Asia and the Middle East. Although it is now a modern manufacturing and service hub, this reflects the enterpot trade role of Singapore which still accounts for close to 40% of Singapore's total trade (Lim, 2004). Logistics is very well developed in Singapore and a lion's share of the trade between South Asia and East Asia passes through Singapore. Many South Asian countries view Singapore as a good secondary base to maintain some of their operations for overseas including those in PRC and other ASEAN countries.

In its efforts to develop its service sector further, Singapore is increasingly emerging as the knowledge hub for Asian economic integration. This can be assessed from the activities of think tanks in the country and the conferences that are organized on the subject. Singapore could also provide technical advice and training to other countries in the region.

END NOTES

Akamatsu, K (1962). Historical pattern of economic growth in developing countries. *The Developing Economies*, 1, 3–25.

Francois, J, PB Rana and G Wingaraja (2008 forthcoming). *East Asia-South Asia Economic Relations: The Way Ahead*. Palgrave Macmillan.

Gill, IG and H Kharas (2007). *An East Asian Renaissance: Ideas for Economic Growth*. World Bank, Washington, DC.

Goh, CT (2006). *Towards an East Asian Renaissance*. Address at the opening session of the 4th Asia-Pacific Roundtable organized by the Global

Foundation, the World Bank, and the Institute of Southeast Asian Studies.

IMF Independent Evaluation Office (2003). *The IMF and Recent Capital Account Crisis: Indonesia, Korea, and Brazil.* International Monetary Fund, Washington DC.

Isard, P (2005). *Globalization and the International Financial System.* London: Cambridge University Press.

Kawai, M (2005). East Asian economic regionalism: Progress and challenges. *Journal of Asian Economics*, 16(1), pp. 29–55.

Kawai, M and G Wignaraja (2007). ASEAN+3 or ASEAN+6: Which Way Forward? Asian Development Bank Institute Discussion Paper 77, Tokyo.

Kawai, M and PB Rana (2008 forthcoming). Preparedness for Future Financial Crisis in East Asia: Global, National and Regional Perspectives. London: Routledge.

Lim, CY (2004). *Southeast Asia: The Long Road Ahead.* Singapore: World Scientific.

Mahbubani, K (2008). The New Asian Hemisphere: The Irresistible Shift of Global Power to the East, Public Affairs.

Monetary Authority of Singapore (2007). Asian Financial and Monetary Integration: Challenges and Prospects, Singapore.

Rana, PB (2007). Economic integration and synchronization of business cycles in East Asia. *Journal of Asian Economics*, 18, pp. 711–725.

Rana, PB (2008). Trade intensity and business cycle synchronization: The Case of East Asian Countries. *Singapore Economic Review*, 53(2), pp. 279–292.

Rana, PB and JM Dowling (2008 forthcoming). *South Asia — Rising to the Challenge of Globalization.* Singapore: World Scientific.

Chapter

8

Asia's Role in the Global Economy and the International Financial System

Chia Wai-Mun, Zhang Yang and Yang Bo

SUMMARY

In the past twenty years, globalization has led to increasing connectedness and integration between countries. Asia has utilized this opportunity and enjoyed a continuous rapid economic growth. At the same time, this "double-edged sword" also brought costs and pains to Asia especially in the Asian Financial Crisis.

Having experienced both benefits and costs, it is essential for Asia to identify its role in the global economy and the international financial system, so as to stand at a better position in the following globalization process. In this chapter, we focus on Asia's role in two scenerios.

First, we look at the possibility of Asia in negotiating for a greater role in the international institutions such as International Monetary Fund (IMF) and World Bank. As a result of its rising economic weight in the world economy, Asia needs to negotiate for greater responsibilities and representations in these institutions, so that the region has a larger role to play in the construction of world economic and financial system as well as regional crisis management.

Second, in the event where such negotiation for greater responsibilities failed, we suggest the idea of forming Asia's own independent regional institutions so that the region is responsible for its own economic destiny. We then focus on Asia's role in the new era of world's economy — a tripartite arrangement, in which the world consists of three major regional blocks, namely, the US, EU and Asia. We identify a few areas in which Asian countries should work on in the process of forming the block, and also discuss the challenges and obstacles ahead.

INTRODUCTION

Globalization, a process that has led to increasing connectedness and integration between countries, has accelerated since the mid-twentieth century. Countries have become more closely connected as evident in increasing flows of goods and services, financial resources and technology transfers across national borders. On the trade side, globalization leads countries to many significant benefits which include lower-priced goods and broader variety of goods to consumers. On the capital side, globalization allows international capital flows to finance production facilities in countries where labor is relatively abundant and capital is relatively scarce. Like many other countries, Asia[1] receives significant economic benefits from the process of greater economic integration. For instance, its purchasing power parity output has surged from US$4,242 billion in 1986 to US$22,274 billion in 2006 and its trade with the rest of the world has increased by 7 times within the 20 years.

[1] For the purpose of this study, unless otherwise stated, Asia includes the ten members of ASEAN, Japan, China, South Korea and India. The ten members of ASEAN are Brunei, Cambodia, Indonesia, Laos, Malaysia, Myanmar, Philippines, Singapore, Thailand and Vietnam.

Nevertheless, the process of globalization has also disrupted the economic circumstances of many people. On the trade side, it widens income gaps between rich and poor countries along with rising inequality and poverty within countries. On the capital side, it has been viewed as a source of destabilization when large volumes of capital inflows are followed by sharp capital decelerations and reversals, and more importantly the effects are highly contagious in which a financial crisis in one country triggers substantial financial market turbulence in other countries. With all these arguments in mind, although the benefits of globalization are recognized, it comes with very high costs. However, an attempt to turn back the clock of this process can be too disturbing and damaging. The magnitude of destruction may be of equivalent to the kind associated with the protectionist and inward-looking beggar-thy-neighbor policies that contributed to the 1930s' Great Depression. In other words, there is a constant risk of a setback towards protectionism if the world trading system and the world financial system do not continue to liberalize.

From these perspectives, while identifying Asia's role in the global economy and the international financial system, the key challenge is to devise effective ways for national policymakers, regional agencies, and international institutions to address problems associated with greater economic integration. In other words, the task is to identify the role of Asia in strengthening national, regional and international institutions for greater economic stability and success in the process of integration and globalization.

In this chapter, we focus on the need to negotiate for greater responsibilities of Asia in international institutions commensurate with its growing economic weight. This is particularly true with the rise of China since 1980s and recently, India. A failure in such negotiation will imply the consideration of forming its own independent regional institutions so that the region is responsible for its own economic destiny. The analysis is made by limiting the attention to the role of Asia in economic welfare, ignoring considerations in the issues related to environment, the stability of cultures and political systems.

1. AN OVERVIEW OF ASIA'S DEVELOPMENT

The aggregate economy and external trade with the rest of the world have grown in volumes which are as large as those of the US and the EU. As shown in Table 1, the purchasing power parity (PPP) output of Asia has improved from US$4,242 billion to US$22,274 billion from 1986 to 2006. On the other hand, the current price output has increased from US$2,911 billion to US$10,006 billion.

In terms of the PPP output in Asia, China has demonstrated the most impressive improvement since 1980 where the output has been raised by more that tenfold. This can be seen clearly from Fig. 1.

1.1. Trade in Goods

External trade in Asia has increased by 776 percent where trade with the rest of the world is US$700 billion in 1986 and is US$6,135 billion in 2006. The rise in external trade in Asia is partly contributed by the improved trade performance of ASEAN and India.

With the accelerating process of globalization, volume of trade has increased substantially in the three regions. This is particularly true for Asia and the EU. From Fig. 2, it can seen that volume of trade has increased drastically after 1985.

Table 1: Output in 1986 and 2006

	Output, ($bn) (PPP)		Output, ($bn) (Current Price)	
	1986	2006	1986	2006
ASEAN + 3* + India	4,242	22,274	2,911	10,006
EU-15	4,620	12,467	3,834	13,610
United States	4,463	13,195	4,463	13,195

* ASEAN+3 excludes Brunei, Cambodia and Laos but includes China, Japan and South Korea.
Source: Economic Intelligent Unit Country Data.

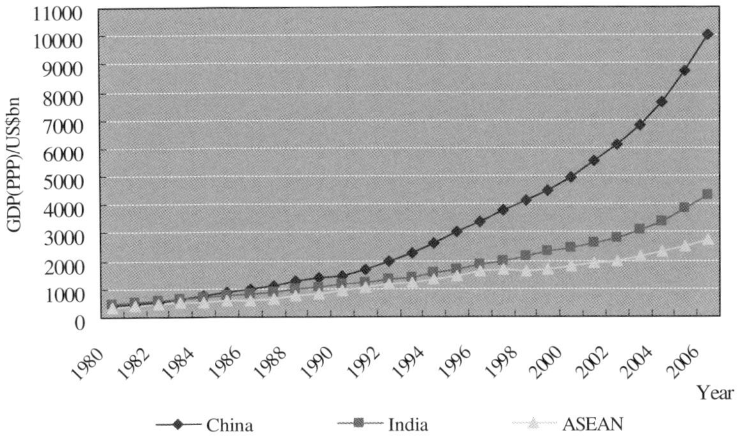

Source: Economic Intelligent Unit Country Data.

Figure 1: GDP of China, India and ASEAN

Table 2: Trade of Asia with the rest of the world in 1986 and 2006

	Trade with the rest of the world ($bn)		
	1986	2006	Change (%)
ASEAN + 3 + India	700	6,135	776
ASEAN	156	1,661	967
China, Japan & Korea	514	4,023	683
India	30	450	1,379
EU-15	2,106	10,426	395
United States	774	3,697	378

Source: Economic Intelligent Unit Country Data.

1.2. Accumulation of Foreign Reserves

Total reserve by Asia has increased drastically from US$91 billion in 1986 to US$2,717 billion in 2006 which is approximately a 2,885 percent increase (as shown in Table 3).

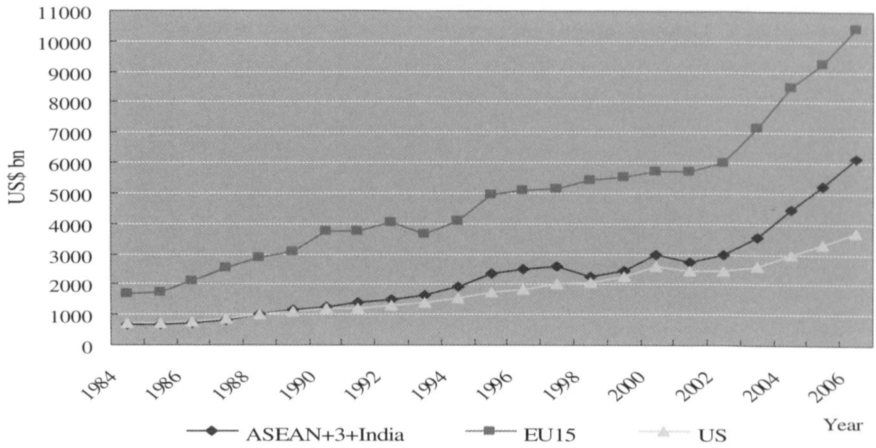

Source: Economic Intelligent Unit Country Data.

Figure 2: Volume of trade from Asia, the EU and the US

Table 3: Official monetary reserve in 1986 and 2006

	Official monetary reserve ($bn)		
	1986	2006	Change (%)
Asia & India	91	2,717	2,885
EU-15	280	483	72
United States	37	55	47

Source: Economic Intelligent Unit Country Data.

The painful experience during the Asian Financial Crisis has led to an interesting observation of a greater rate of reserve accumulation.

Since 1997, Asia has decided that it does not want to be dependent on the West or global financial institutions, in particular the IMF, when trouble hits again in future. Countries in the region clearly realize that international institutions on which they were previously dependent on are no longer reliable. Figure 3 shows that the total reserve in Asia has increased drastically after the region regained its economic strengths.

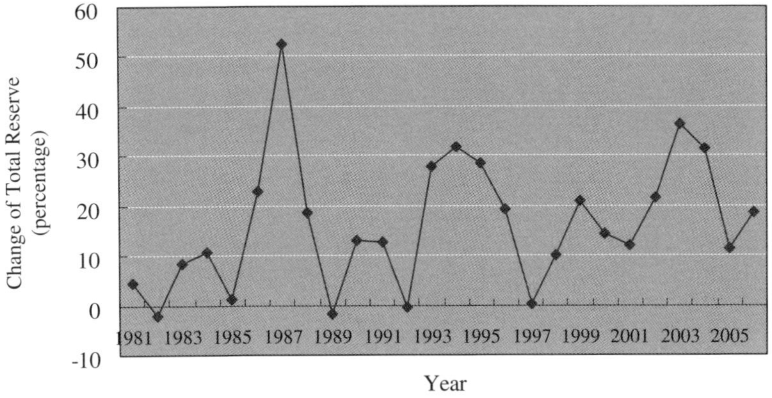

Source: Economic Intelligent Unit Country Data.

Figure 3: Percentage change of total reserve in Asia

2. REPRESENTATION AT WORLD INSTITUTIONS

As the region regains more economic strength, it gives rise to two distinct but not unrelated directions to the policymakers in the region. First, Asia should take on greater responsibilities commensurate with its growing economic weight. This suggests that Asia should have a larger role in international financial institutions and groupings such as the IMF and the World Bank. Second, in the event of its failure to negotiate for greater responsibilities at the international institutions, Asia should request for institutions of its own so that the countries have a central control of its own destiny.

As shown in Table 1 and Fig. 1, since Asia (1) accounts for a large proportion of global gross domestic product measured in terms of purchasing power parity, (2) has the majority of global reserve, along with the fact that (3) the region has the majority of the world's population, the countries in the region deserve the right to ask for adequate representation in both the IMF and the World Bank. Table 4 serves to illustrate the imbalance between Asia's output and its representation in the IMF.

Table 4 shows the GDP, percentage of staff and percentage of voting power in the IMF of the three major economic blocks in the

Table 4: Comparison of three regions in output and IMF representation

	GDP (US$bn) (PPP)*	Percentage of staff member	Percentage of voting power**
Asia	22,274	15.7	16.13
EU	12,467	28	29.21
US	13,195	23.9	16.79
Percentage of Asia Among the three	46.47%	23.22%	25.96%

Notes: * data for year 2006; ** by January 04, 2008
Source: Economic Intelligent Unit Country Data;
IMF website: http://www.imf.org/external/np/sec/memdir/members.htm#total

world. In terms of GDP (purchasing power parity), Asia contributed 46.47% among the three regions. However, the representation of Asia in the IMF is almost only half of its share in output. The imbalance of staff members is even more severe when it comes to the higher positions.

Thus, an increase in representation should come in the form of larger number of staff and key positions as well as the voting power.

Even though the G20 of the world's leading rich and developing countries has called for reform in the international institutions, there may be of little success, as the failure is reflective of the fact that Asia holds limited voting power in these institutions themselves. Countries from Asia need better representation at the international institutions to call for possible governance reform, but this is impossible without governance reform at the first place.

3. A NEW WORLD ARRANGEMENT — A TRIPARTITE WORLD

The most striking change in both the world trading and world financial systems is the emergence of three-block-configuration which can be clearly distinguished into the US, Europe and Asia by the ten members of the ASEAN, China, Japan, South Korea, and soon with India.

The formation of Asia as a new regional block is supported by five basic reasons. First, the experience of the Asian Financial Crisis in 1997 to 1998 suggests that crisis in one country has repercussion effects on other countries in the region. The all-too-evident neighborhood contagion effects give creditor countries strong interest in pooling resources with others to avoid further destruction. Second, the failures of the World Trade Organization (WTO) and the Asia-Pacific Economic Cooperation (APEC) to proceed on trade liberalization lead to the idea of separate arrangement within Asia. Third, Asia is inspired by the success of the European integration especially the Euro. Forth, countries in Asia, in general, are broadly disquieted with the behavior of both the US and the EU. Finally, the difficulties encountered in the negotiation of greater representation at the IMF and the World Bank.

However, with or without larger role in the global institutions, countries in Asia must be determined to devise effective fiscal, monetary and exchange rate policies and accelerate structural adjustments in order to ensure that the region is less vulnerable to any form of financial crisis in the future.

3.1. Asian Monetary Fund

IMF and the G7 group of industrialized countries always recognize themselves of playing key role in the international financial architecture. However, the frustration and disappointment towards the response of the IMF and the US in the Asian Financial Crisis of 1997–1998 is the single greatest catalyst for the proposal of an Asian Monetary Fund (AMF). The AMF was first proposed in August 1997 to deal with the crisis in the region where it managed to secure pledges of US$100 billion from China, Hong Kong, Taiwan and Singapore. The AMF, if successfully formed, will build on Asia's savings surplus, foreign exchange reserves, and net creditor status (including reserves and Treasury bills). This will allow the Asian countries to refinance their loans and provide new loans for recovery programs. It may be of the incentive of the Asian countries to assist other countries in the region when they are hit by a financial crisis as the high degree of economic interdependence within Asia suggests that crisis that hit one country hurts the other countries too. This may give creditor country a strong interest to pool resources together to prevent the contagion effect.

However, there are obstacles and challenges ahead of Asia to materialize the idea of setting up the AMF. These obstacles can be both internal and external.

3.2. Exchange Rate: Fix or Float

In 2000, Lawrence Summers listed 7 somewhat common features of crisis episodes for 7 countries which were badly hurt by financial crisis. These countries include Mexico, Thailand, Indonesia, Malaysia, Korea, Russia and Brazil. These subjective assessments suggest that pegged exchange rates contributed very seriously to the vulnerability of countries to financial crisis.

Fixed exchange rates are by definition central to financial crisis. In 1997, the IMF advised Asian countries to float their currencies. In 1998, it lent to Russia and Brazil so that they could maintain the value of their currencies. It praised Hong Kong for its strict currency board system and distinguished Singapore for its managed float system. The advices seem to be highly inconsistent. Historical experience provides strong evidence that unless countries can control international capital flows, they will not find it possible to stabilize exchange rates between their currencies and simultaneously retain autonomy to utilize their monetary policies to achieve domestic economic growth. This fundamental theorem explains why financial crisis have to become so powerful under the existing international monetary system.

Traditionally, merit is often attributed to flexible exchange rate regimes over fixed exchange rate regimes in their ability to insulate the economy more effectively against real shocks. The presence of price stickiness explains why the exchange rate may matter. When an economy is hit by real shocks, the economy that can then change relative prices more quickly will have smaller and smoother adjustment in output.This is particularly true in an economy with price stickiness where the speed at which relative prices can adjust, depends crucially on the exchange rate regime. Under flexible exchange rate regimes, relative prices can adjust instantly through changes in nominal exchange rate, while under fixed exchange rate regimes, relative prices can adjust only at the speed that is permitted by price stickiness, which is usually much slower.Therefore, flexible exchange rate regimes allow smoother adjustment in output and quicker adjustment in relative prices than fixed exchange rate regimes.

However, flexible exchange rate regimes do have a major drawback i.e., the risk of high volatility.They can overshoot and become highly unstable particularly with large size of international capital flow in and out of the country.This instability has real economic costs as it reduces investors' confidence in one currency and making the task of combating inflation a lot harder.Which is preferred? Most academics find it hard to come to a common consensus. They rarely agree on the best solution. However, in general, they believe that only radical solutions will work i.e., either currency must be left completely free or must be tightly fixed.

With the success of Singapore in managing its exchange rate, a managed float is recommended with the ability of monetary authorities to adjust its currency when necessary.The monetary authorities may choose to set an exchange rate according to a basket of foreign currency based on its trade volumes with the foreign countries. This exchange rate will be allowed to vary within a targeted band. When the exchange rate reaches the upper or lower band, the monetary authorities will intervene. However, there is a key challenge associated with such policy as a continuous re-evaluation mechanism on the actual exchange rate must be established. This actual exchange rate must be determined based on real factors such as volumes of export and imports and perhaps foreign direct investment.

In additional to the suggestion of managed float regime, Asian countries may choose to discourage and restrict short-term capital inflow to minimize currency volatility. Large inflows of capital in Asia help the region in their economic development. This is particularly true if these flows are foreign direct investment. In any other cases, a flow of short-term capital into any economy with immature and poorly regulated financial institutions can be disastrously harmful. Therefore, the best idea to the Asian economies is to impose their own supervisory controls on short-term international borrowing by domestic financial institutions. To prevent massive capital reversals, it is best to prevent financial institutions from exposing themselves to excess short-term indebtedness.

3.3. Capital Control vs. Capital Liberalization

Bitter experiences for many Asian countries during the Asian Financial Crisis, direct governments in the region to learn a meaningful lesson. Large inflows of foreign capital present them with irresistible opportunity to accelerate their economic development. When these inflows of foreign capital are for long-term direct investment, they are beneficial. For instance, foreign direct investment in new productive assets of a country will bring economic benefits such as growth and employment. However, in any other cases, heavy inflows of short-term financial capital into an economy without matured and properly regulated financial institutions can do more harm than good.

With this argument in mind, should capital be controlled? Generally, any controls, from a free market economics perspective, will be oppressive to citizens and economically harmful. Additionally, measures to block capital outflows, will deter future inflows of all kinds including good capital inflows. Therefore, measures to control capital will perhaps serve only as an option at time of crisis and countries that use capital control in the event of crisis have to trade-off its short-term benefits of preventing capital outflows from the costs of future credibility.

3.4. Common Currency

A common currency in Asia is an attractive idea in many years, especially after the success of Euros. According to optimum currency area theory developed by Mundell Mckinnon and Kenen, to determine the appropriateness of a group of countries in forming optimum currency area, a number of criteria have to be satisfied. These criteria include (1) degree of similarity in business cycles and shocks, (2) degree of openness, (3) degree of factor mobility internationally, and (4) degree of product differentiation. This idea though attractive, seems implausible for Asia at the current period not only because of the difficulties in meeting such theoretical requirements but also its practical economic and political obstacles as discussed in the following section.

4. OBSTACLES AND CHALLENGES AHEAD

When Asia is moving towards a more integrated regional block, there are challenges and obstacles ahead. First, the countries within Asia are significantly different in terms of cultures, political systems and levels of economic development. Second, most of these countries even though are institutionally linked through ASEAN (one way or another) for more than 30 years continue to perceive each other as competitors rather than partners. Even though, as identified, Asia may benefit significantly from regional currency stability, national sentiments and mutual suspicion, especially between China and Japan, may rule out the possibility of setting up either the Asian Monetary Fund (AMF) or any form of regional unions. Third, obstacles and pressures may arise from the West for Asia going its own way. For instance, when the AMF was first proposed in 1997 with the objective of dealing with the financial crisis in Asia, the US killed the proposal and it died. According to their explanation, the IMF should be the only coordinator of the rescue effort.

5. CONCLUSIONS

The world is getting more closely connected but yet divided. This may appear contradicting but not without its justification. Advances in communication and transportation have provided a major driving force of international economic integration. From this perspective, the world is getting more closely connected. Countries trade more in terms of goods and capital. Volumes of import and export of goods and services, and capital flows, have increased drastically in the past few decades. The consequences of such economic integration are visible. Consumers benefit from lower-price goods. Producers benefit from the spread of technological and marketing know-how. While enjoying the fruits of globalization, many countries are getting together to make their own economic arrangements. In both the trading and financial systems, the world is becoming a three-block configuration which comprises of the US, the EU and Asia.

Many Asian governments are interested to request for greater responsibilities in international institutions commensurate with the rising economic weight of Asia in the world economy. As Asia accounts for a larger global GDP, a larger global reserve and a larger population, the region serves the right to ask for sufficient representation at the global institutions or else they may be losing their significance. However, such request requires a call for governance reforms at these institutions which may be of little success. This is because Asia needs better representation at the international institutions to call for possible governance reform but this is impossible without governance reform at the first place. In this chapter we suggest that in the event of failure in solving such a "chicken and egg" problem, countries from Asia may like to choose another alternative of forming their own new regional block so that they could be the masters of their own fate.

Additionally, since an attempt to turn back the clock of globalization can be disturbing and damaging, a sounder basis for globalization is of urgent need. The key issue is perhaps for the IMF and the World Bank to be aware of their role as development and financial plumbers to connect not only Asia, but Russia, Africa and Latin America back to the world economy. The key issue is then to help devise effective ways for national policy makers and international agencies to address the problems and challenges associated with further economic integration, from both international trade and international finance.

Chapter

9

Globalization, Income Polarization and the Rise of the "New Challengers"

Shubhasree Seshanna

Globalization, the progressive integration of the world economy, has reached unprecedented levels, surpassing the peak levels attained before the First World War. It is a very complex and multi-faceted process, and is affecting the economic well-being of people around the world. Globalization has happened before; starting around 1870, trade, migration and capital flows reached unprecedented levels (until now), driven mainly by declining transportation costs. While, at the time, it seemed that globalization was inevitable, it was the first wave that was followed by a retreat into nationalism and protectionism, two World Wars and the Great Depression. Only after 1945 did we see a return to patterns similar to those of the first wave. This integration was mainly confined to the rich economies of the world. The third (current) wave of globalization started around 1980 marked an important change — many developing economies, "the new globalizers" broke into world markets for manufactures rather than primary commodities.

CHARACTERISTICS OF THE LATEST WAVE OF GLOBALIZATION

Some important distinctive characteristics of this new wave of globalization include, first, the emergence of a large group of developing countries as global producers of non-primary products and services (sometimes called "globalization from below"). The populations of these countries number around 3 billion, according to the World Bank. By taking advantage of their labor abundance, and supported by reasonably good policies, infrastructure and institutions, these countries, by and large, have seen large reductions in poverty and high rates of growth.

The second feature of this new wave of globalization is that, countries with a population of around 2 billion, have not integrated into the global economy. They include several countries in Africa and the former Soviet Union. Professor Paul Collier, of Oxford University, draws attention in his new book, to the fact that nearly a billion people are still trapped in the depths of poverty (Sachs, 2006; Collier, 2007). Most of what he dubs the "bottom billion" lives in 58 countries, 70% of them in Africa and most of the rest in Central Asia.[1] Since the 1990s, around 4 billion poor people worldwide have started to move out of absolute poverty, some of them very rapidly and most spectacularly in East Asia (Alesina, 1991; Barro, 1991, 1992).

The current wave of globalization appears inevitable, desirable and also frightening. Kofi Annan, former head of the United Nations, expresses a sense of inevitability, "... arguing against globalization is like arguing against the laws of gravity". In a similar vein, former US President Bill Clinton calls globalization "... the economic equivalent of a force of nature — like wind or water". A lot of the debate on the benefits of globalization centers on the impact of globalization, the distributional of income (Lindert, 2001; Mankiw, 1992; Persson, 1994; Seshanna, 2003; Stiglitz, 2007). Economist, Paul Samuelson cautions,

[1] Dr. Collier explains, "in one or more of four traps — wars, in which 73% of the poorest have been caught at one time or another; natural resources gone wrong (Nigeria and its oil), which accounts for about 30%; landlocked with bad neighbors (Chad); and the bad-governance-in-a-small-country trap (too many to name)".

"Globalization presumes sustained economic growth. Otherwise, the process loses its economic benefits and political support". Skeptical about its distributional impact, former US President, Jimmy Carter, points out that "if you're totally illiterate and living on one dollar a day, the benefits of globalization never come to you".

Many studies agree that for the successful globalizers, overall incomes have risen (Dollar and Kray, 2001b). World incomes have risen on average as well. Some assert that world income inequality is rising, as inequality within countries. World income inequality depends on both between-country and within-country inequality. The evidence on the trends in within-country inequality has been mixed. At the household level, studies such as Ravallion (2001) show that growth benefits the poor, but the resulting decrease in inequality can vary greatly across countries. In one paper, Dollar and Kraay (2001a, 2001b) find that trade liberalization (increased volumes and lowered tariffs) leads to economic growth which itself benefits the poor by lowering absolute poverty; but there seems to be no effect on inter-country inequality. In other words, growth benefits the poor as much as it benefits the average household. In another paper, O'Rourke (2001) finds that, even if historically between-countries inequality increased for the past 200 years, the trend may turn around soon.

This chapter focuses solely on between-country comparisons. It first examines the trend identified above, the unprecedented participation of developing economies in the world industrial economy, with particular emphasis on the emergence of multinationals from developing countries. Then it looks at the question of whether globalization has increased the global income divide between the successful globalizers and the unsuccessful ones. In the light of the World Bank's results, which show 3 billion people successfully integrating into the world economy and 2 billion people being left out, the concept that best captures the global divide between the two groups is not just income inequality but income *polarization*. Polarization, though related to inequality, is a distinct concept, denoting a particular type of change in the income distribution — a movement of the observations from the middle of the distribution towards the two tails or a "hollowing of the middle" of the distribution, or associated with a "tendency towards bimodality" (Foster, 1992; Wolfson, 1994; Quah, 1996). The Wolfson index of polarization is used in this analysis.[2] Wolfson (1994, 1997) points out that standard inequality measures may not distinguish the increased polarization of a distribution from other kinds of changes in the distribution (say a lengthening of the lower tail). He also shows that sometimes the two measures may disagree. In the context of inter-country income distribution, polarization would mean a greater concentration of the low-income and high-income countries, at the expense of those in the middle. This chapter, therefore, looks not only at trends in inter-country inequality but also inter-country polarization.

THE RISE OF THE "NEW CHALLENGERS"

We are witnessing what amounts to a revolution in the way world production is undertaken. Companies from developing countries such as China, India, Brazil, Russia Mexico and Turkey are expanding rapidly overseas and going global. The world has woken up to the arrival of these emerging market multinationals. Thanks to some huge deals that attracted media attention. These cases include expatriate Indian business Mittal's bid for the European steelmaker Arcelor, the battle between two Indian firms, Tata and Mahindra and Mahindra over Jaguar, China's Lenovo's purchase of IBM's PC business, and Tata's battle with Brazil's CSN for Corus, an Anglo-Dutch steel maker. The well-known Indian trio of Wipro, Infosys and Tata Consultancy Services (TCS) has built an IT outsourcing industry that is challenging industry leaders such as Accenture and IBM. China's BYD Company is now the world's largest producer of nickel-cadmium batteries, and China's home appliance makers Haier and Hisense are very big in Europe, Cemex from Mexico is one of the

---

[2] The polarization index is given by: $P = (T - Gini/2)/mtan$, where $T = 0.5 - L(0.5)$ is the difference between 50 percent and the income share of the bottom half of the population (which latter, is referred to as the "median share"), and $mtan = median/mean$. See Wolfson (1994), for details.

world's largest producers of cement, Brazil's Embraer has become the market leader in regional jets, overtaking Canada's Bombardier, China's Chery Automobile, the leading car exporter plans to build plants in Eastern Europe, the Middle East and South America and India's Bharat Forge is now the world's second-largest forging company. While these prominent examples get all the attention, several thousand such companies are actively trying to expand abroad.

A 2006 study by the Boston Consulting Group (BCG), found 100 companies from emerging markets with total assets of US$520 billion that year.[3] By 2004, the United Nations Conference on Trade and Development (UNCTAD) had noted that five companies from emerging Asia had made it into the world's biggest multinational companies (MNCs) and ten made it into the top 200.[4] Furthermore, Foreign Direct Investment (FDI) from developing countries (including mergers and acquisitions) in 2006 was US$174 billion (14% of the world's total). Now we are seeing a new and fundamental shift, investment is increasingly flowing from *South to North* and from *South to South* as these new MNCs invest in both the rich and the developing world. The BRICs (a term coined by Goldman Sachs in 2003 to denote the largest globalizing countries, Brazil, Russia, India and China) in particular, feature predominantly in the list of the top 100 multinationals from the developing world (see Fig. 1).

According to BCG, thousands of such companies are expanding sales and production internationally. They are not simply exporters but are setting up plants in many countries of the world. They have certain advantages in their home markets, such as rapid economic growth, low costs, and cheap state finance. Moreover, managers have learned to be adaptable and resilient in an environment full of difficulties in operation. The gradual liberalization of these countries has exposed these firms to competition from global incumbents form rich countries.

---

[3] These 100 "global challengers" exclude Singaporean companies.

[4] The UNCTAD began its analysis in the 1970s when Europe felt threatened by the likes of IBM and General Motors, and noted in the 1980s that the United States was worried about the inroads Japanese firms were making into America.

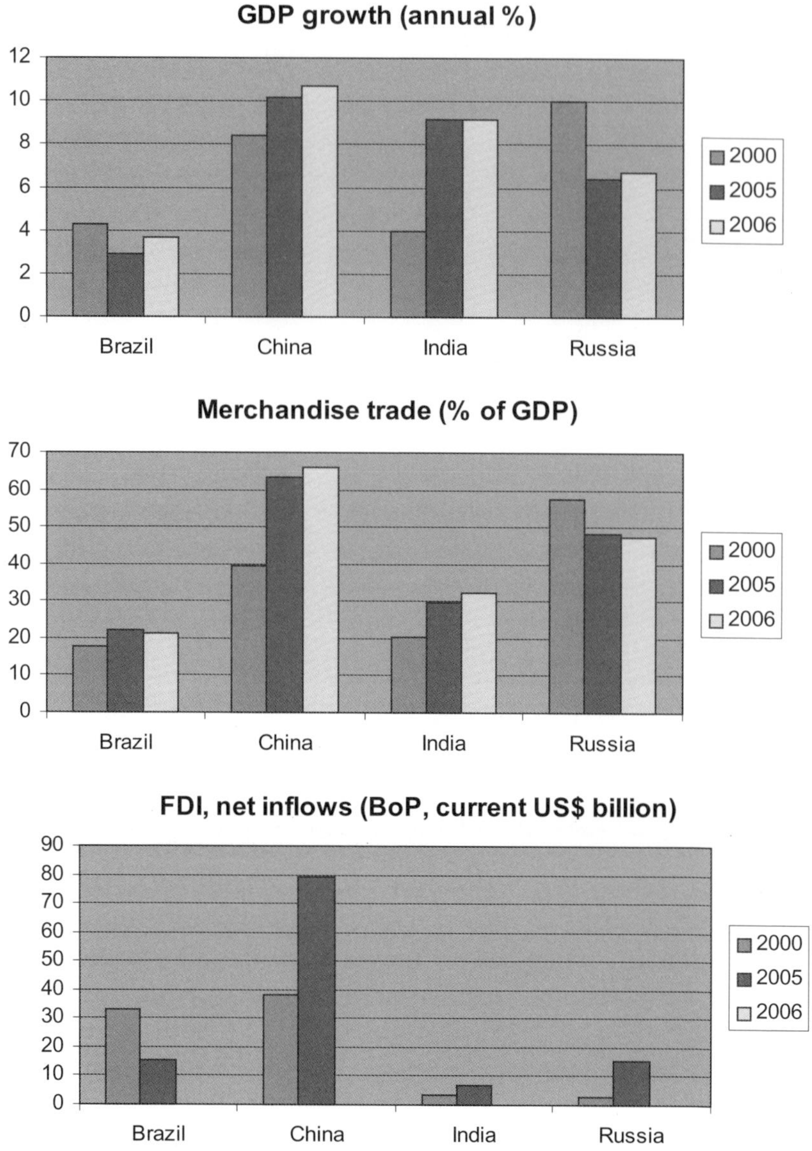

Source: Derived from World Bank data.

Figure 1: Some variables of interest (Brazil, Russia, India and China)

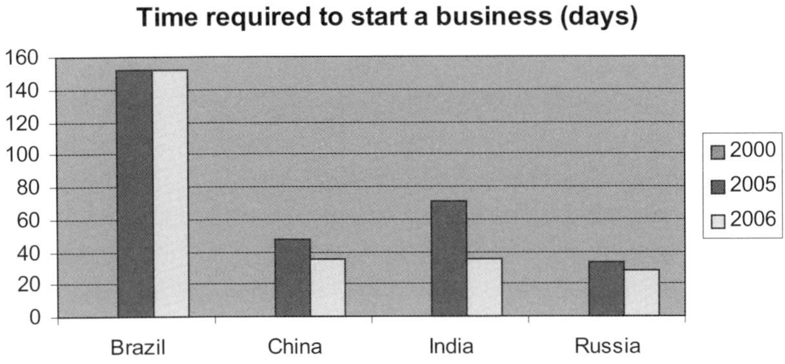

Figure 1: *(Continued)*

The BCG study also finds that of the 100 top companies[5] from what they call "Rapidly Developing Countries" (RDE), that are on "the leading edge of globalizing their businesses", 70 are from Asia (44 Chinese and 21 Indian), 18 from Latin America (12 from Brazil, 6 from Mexico) and another 12 from Egypt, Russia and Turkey. Most of the Chinese companies are state-controlled/owned, only one Indian company is. The "RDE 100" produce industrial goods (32), consumer durables (18), resource extraction (15), food-and-beverage and cosmetics (11), technology equipment (6) and others such as pharmaceuticals, mobile-communications, shipping and infrastructure (18). Table 1 presents the top ten companies and Table 2 presents selected companies that make it to the top 100.

Five strategies used by these companies were identified by BCG. The first is taking brands form local to global. A good example is China's Hisense, a consumer-electronics group, with a 10% market share at home, has manufacturing plants in several countries and sells television sets and air-conditioners in over 40 countries. Another example is India's Bajaj Auto, exports three- and two-wheelers, mostly to South-East Asia.

A second strategy is turning local engineering talent into global innovation, as Embraer of Brazil has done. Combining low-cost

[5] Excluding Singaporean Companies.

Table 1: Top ten emerging global multinationals*

Rank	Company	Country
1	Aluminum Corporation of China (Chalco)	China
2	América Móvil	Mexico
3	Bajaj Auto	India
4	Bharat Forge	India
5	BOE Technology Group Company	China
6	Braskem	Brazil
7	BYD Company	China
8	Cemex	Mexico
9	Charoen Pokphand Foods	Thailand
10	China Aviation Corporation	China

* Excluding Singaporean Companies.
Source: Boston Consulting Group.

Table 2: Selected emerging global multinationals*

Rank	Company	Country
15	China Mobile	China
18	China Petroleum & Chemical Corporation	China
21	Cipla	India
22	CNOOC	China
23	Companhia Vale do Rio Duce (CVRD)	Brazil
30	Embraer	Brazil
35	Gazprom	Russia
39	Grupo Modelo	Mexico
44	Indofood Sukses Makmur	Indonesia
47	Koç Holding	Turkey
50	Lukoil	Russia
53	Malaysia International Shipping Company	Malaysia
66	Petronas	Malaysia
84	Thai Union Frozen Products	Thailand
99	Wipro	India

* Excluding Singaporean Companies.
Source: Boston Consulting Group.

manufacturing with advanced R&D, it is now world leader in regional jets, with 95% of its sales outside Brazil.

A third method used by these companies is striving for global leadership in a narrow product category. China's BYD Company, the battery-maker, and Hong Kong's Johnson Electric, electric motor maker, have followed this route.

The fourth strategy used by Brazil's Sadia and Perdigão (pork and poultry producers), for e.g., is to take advantage of natural resources in the home country, along with excellent marketing and distribution.

The fifth and final strategy is to have a new or better business model, which is then rolled out in many different markets. This is the approach used by Mexico's cement producer, Cemex, now the world's biggest supplier of ready-mix concrete.

These "new challengers" do have some advantages; they are often family-owned or family-controlled, which help them decide quickly, and they get cheap finance from state banks. But they also face many problems, trying to break into a world economy that is already globalized and dominated by some powerful incumbents. This has not deterred many of them from taking advantage of opportunities presented to them by globalization.

It is interesting to note that the large East Asian economies of Malaysia, Indonesia, Thailand and the Philippines are not as well-represented in the BCG 100 as one would expect (there is no global name similar to Korea's LG, for example), despite a good recovery from the 1997 financial crisis, several years of strong growth and improved government finances. Singapore is an exception and the region's most advanced economy. Singapore Airlines is the region's most recognizable brand, and also the fourth largest international carrier. Keppel and SembCorp are the world's two largest producers of offshore oil drilling-rigs. Some of Singapore's tech firms like Chartered Semiconductors and Creative are facing strong competition from Taiwan. The region has produced some important banks, Singapore's OCBC and Malaysia's Public Bank, which are also expanding beyond their borders. But here again, they have to contend with Western and Chinese banks. Also of some concern is that unlike Korea's and Taiwan's export-led growth, which came from home-grown firms making globally competitive products, South-East Asian firms depend a lot on high-value exports made by foreign companies. This makes them vulnerable to the risk that the company will move to a lower cost destination.

WHAT ARE THE IMPLICATIONS FOR THE INCUMBENT FIRMS OF THE RISE OF THE "CHALLENGERS"?

The competition the incumbents are facing and will continue to face will raise the stakes of the game. They will have to identify and learn about the challenger firms, and be aware of the new reality of the environment they are operating in. They may choose to compete head-on with the competitors, or cooperate with them and form partnerships and other ties. The number of emerging market companies, though dominated by the two largest economies, China and India at the moment, is likely to keep increasing. Any global company must be prepared to be a major player not only in the rich economies of the world, but also in the rapidly developing world.

Labor productivity in India and China is growing faster than in South-East Asia (IMF, 2007). Firms in South-East Asia must offer more than low wage-costs and they must produce better-qualified workers and innovate more to stay ahead. There are some good performers, Malaysia's YTL conglomerate, Genting and Air Asia, Singapore's Banyan Tree, and Thailand's Bumrungrad hospitals (for "medical tourism"). While the rise of China and India may make it difficult to become large manufacturers, still there are possibilities of producing world-class firms in other areas, such as tourism and hospitality and natural resources (palm oil for Malaysia and Indonesia, rice for Vietnam and Thailand, fish and seafood for Vietnam and Thailand).

INCOME INEQUALITY AND INCOME POLARIZATION OF WORLD INCOMES

This section examines whether the more globalized economies have experienced higher rates of growth than the less globalized, and whether this has been accompanied by increases in inter-country polarization (using the Wolfson measure) and inequality (using the Gini coefficient). A range of measures of openness is used to identify the "globalizers" (or more globalized economies), including membership in the World Trade Organization, tariff rates, and the ratio of trade to GDP. The list of post-1980 globalizers includes some well-known reformers such as Argentina, China, Hungary, India, Malaysia, Mexico, the Philippines and Thailand, and well over half the population of the developing world (see Table 3). The "globalizers" are not drawn from the richer developing economies. In fact, in 1980, they were as a group, poorer than average (they include India and China, massive and poor). Many of the recent globalizers have experienced increased growth rates from the 1970s onwards, while the "non-globalizing" developing countries saw a decline in the average growth rate from the 1970s to the 1980s, and then recovering slightly in the 1990s (Dollar and Kraay, 2001a; World Bank, 2007).

The key variable used is PPP-adjusted real GDP per capita in order to correct for inflation, population size and exchange rates. Note that, to compare one country with another, it is necessary to express the real GDP per capita in a common currency (USD); but exchange rates can create distortions in common prices as well. To prevent such a distortion, the purchasing power parity (PPP) approach is preferred.

The USD PPP adjusted real GDP per capita values came from a core dataset called the Penn World Table (Mark 6.2) denoted PWT 6.2, covering the years from 1980 to 2004 (Heston, 1991, 2006).[6] Countries were then divided into five groups, "globalizers", "non-globalizers", the "world", "East Asia (including China)" and East Asia (excluding China)". As mentioned earlier, the list of post-1980 globalizers includes well over half of the population of the developing world. East Asia is of particular interest, since until about ten years ago, it was the world's fastest-growing region (see Fig. 1 below). For each of these groups three variables are graphed over time. They are mean real GDP per capita, the Gini coefficient and the Wolfson polarization measure.

---

[6] The Penn World Table provides purchasing power parity and national income accounts converted to international prices for 188 countries for some or all of the years 1950–2004.

Table 3: Globalizers

Country	Trade Globalizer	Tariffs Globalizer
Argentina	Yes	Yes
Bangladesh	Yes	Yes
Benin	No	Yes
Brazil	Yes	Yes
Burkina Faso	No	Yes
Cameroon	No	Yes
Central African Republic	No	Yes
China	Yes	Yes
Colombia	Yes	Yes
Costa Rica	Yes	No
Dominican Republic	Yes	No
Ecuador	No	Yes
Egypt, Arab Republic	No	Yes
Haiti	Yes	No
India	Yes	Yes
Indonesia	No	Yes
Ivory Coast	Yes	No
Jamaica	Yes	No
Jordan	Yes	No
Kenya	No	Yes
Malaysia	Yes	No
Mali	Yes	No
Mexico	Yes	No
Nepal	Yes	No
Nicaragua	Yes	Yes
Pakistan	No	Yes
Paraguay	Yes	No
Peru	No	Yes
Philippines	Yes	No
Rwanda	Yes	No
Thailand	Yes	Yes
Uganda	No	Yes
Uruguay	Yes	Yes
Venezuela, RB	No	Yes
Zambia	No	Yes
Zimbabwe	Yes	No

Note: The above table lists the countries that qualify as post-1980 globalizers in terms of increased trade volumes and tariffs reductions (Dollar and Kraay, 2001a). Non-globalizers are the rest of the world (neither increased trade volumes nor tariffs reductions as for the globalizers above), less the OECD countries.

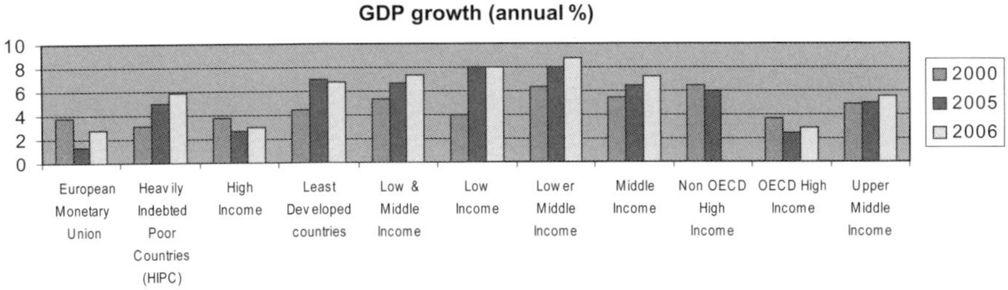

Figure 1: GDP growth rates (2000–2006) derived from World Bank data

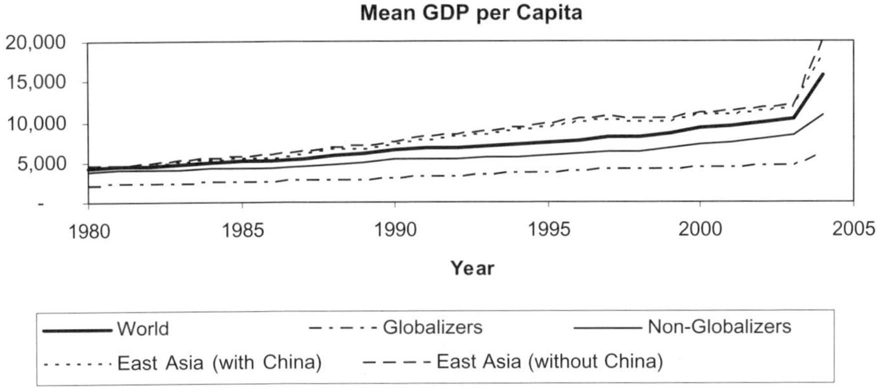

Figure 2: Real mean GDP per capita for different groups (PPP adjusted)

As Fig. 2 shows, real mean GDP per capita of the various groups of countries has followed a fairly continuous and smooth upward trend for all groups concerned, with a significant increase from 2002 onwards. East Asia (with and without the inclusion of China) has remained above the world average throughout, and continues the trend up to 2004. Both the "globalizers" and the "non-globalizers" have real mean GDP per capita below the world average, but the trend is the same for all groups. This is not surprising, as mentioned earlier, the globalizers were not a high-income group of developing countries to start with, in fact, they were poorer than average.

Looking at inequality trends, within-group Gini coefficients are the highest and rising for the world and for the non-globalizers

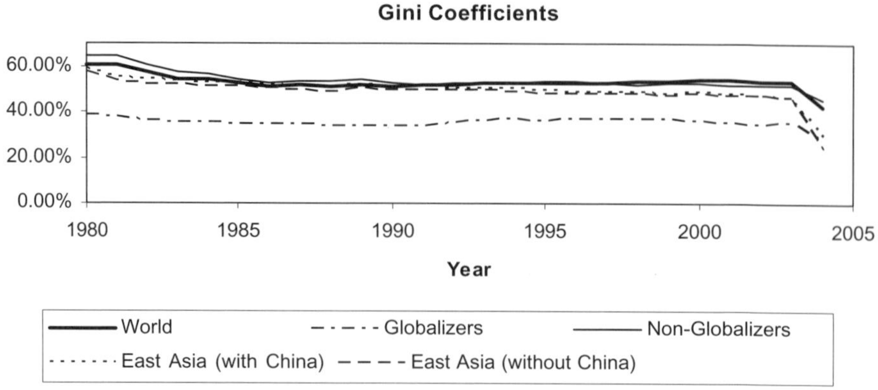

Figure 3: Income inequality across countries and groups (1980–2004)

(see Fig. 3). This makes intuitive sense since all countries are pooled into one group (the world) without any exclusion, thus creating the most heterogeneous group of countries. The Gini coefficient shows a slow decline from 1980–1989, followed by a rise until 2003, after which it dips significantly for all groups. Unfortunately, the dataset ends in 2004, or else, it would have been possible to see if this trend continues further. It is in partial agreement with O'Rourke (2001), who also found an increasing between-country world inequality using the Theil index (Bourguignon and Morrisson, 1999). According to the graph, the globalizers have the lowest within-group Gini, followed by East Asia, and then the "world" and the non-globalizers. The globalizer group is significantly less unequal than the world and the non-globalizing group. East Asian Gini coefficients are consistently below the world average. This would suggest that globalizers and East Asian countries are becoming more equal among themselves within their group. The sharp reduction in inequality in 2003–2004, is in agreement with the IMF's World Economic Outlook (2007) which finds that "trade globalization is not found to have a negative impact on income distribution" in either developed or developing countries.

In the case of polarization, we see some interesting patterns. (Fig. 4) East Asia (including China) is the most polarized group, followed by East Asia (excluding China), the "world", the "non-globalizers"

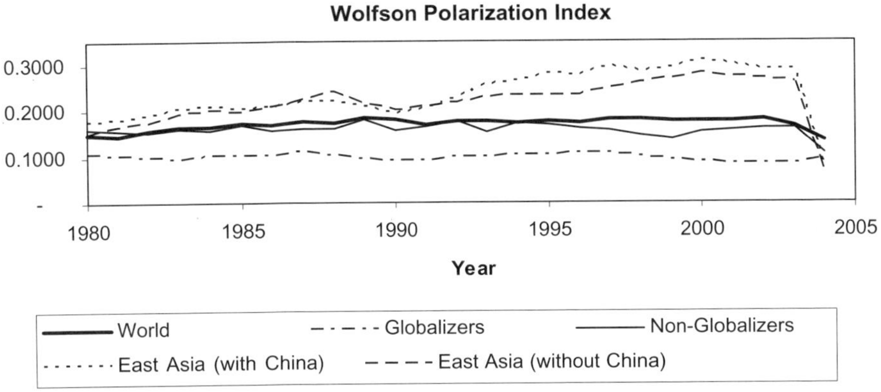

Figure 4: Income polarization of income across countries and groups (1980–2004)

and finally, the "globalizers". The OECD is the only group to show a declining trend in intra-group polarization. In fact, the two East Asian groups are not only more polarized than average, but the level of polarization increases from the late 1980s to the about 2003, after which it drops sharply. The "globalizers" show not only the lowest levels of intra-group polarization, but also a more or less steady declining trend, even in the 1990s. The "non-globalizers" are less polarized than the world or the East Asian groups and also follow a somewhat declining trend. The East Asian groups and the "world" did becoming more polarized especially in the 1990s, but in 2003 onwards the trend appears to reverse itself. This is consistent with more pessimistic studies that worried about a widening economic divide (Stiglitz, 2003), and appears to contradict the optimists who believe the world playing field was getting more equal with time (Friedman, 2005; Bhagwati, 2004). Since polarization appears to reduce after 2003, more time and more data are needed to confirm if the optimists were right after all.

CONCLUSION

The rise of the new challengers from booming domestic markets in developing countries is going to continue. By 2050, China and

India are predicted to be two of the world's three largest economies (BCG, 2006). They are already making the largest contributions in PPP terms to world growth (IMF, 2008). Global companies will become major players not only in North America, Europe and Japan, but also in India, China and other fast-growing economies. South-East Asian firms will have to work harder at innovating and producing better-educated workers to compete in this new environment.

Gini index starts declining between 1980 (the beginning of "globalization" for many) and 1990, after which it follows an upward trend until 2003, when it decreases again. The polarization index, which shows a steady upward trend most of the time, also decreases in 2003–2004. The world was indeed becoming more polarized during the 1980s and 1990s as many believed. However this trend appears to be reversing from 2003 onwards. The "middle" of the distribution is getting "fatter", or more countries are moving closer to the middle of the distribution.

Globalization is creating winners and losers everywhere. Those with the skills and the resources to make use of the opportunities afforded by trade, transnational corporations, Asia (generally speaking), BRICs, some other "emerging economies" (around 24 countries containing 3 billion people) are better off. Those without resources or skills needed (even in East Asia and in the rich world), some Sub-Saharan African countries (though some are growing faster), some ex-Soviet states (in all nearly 2 billion), national governments, the environment and (some) workers in the rich world, are marginalized. Furthermore, migration pressures are building (since the movement of labor is not as free as it was during the first wave of globalization), and more South-North as well as South-South will rise.

There is chance of a rich-country backlash against globalization. Some people in rich countries do lose out from the combination of trade and technology. Many argue (including the IMF) that trade is a much smaller factor than technology. The remedy lies with education and training, and with help in changing jobs — not in efforts to hold back either technological progress or trade.

END NOTES

Alesina, A and D Rodrick (1991). Distributive Politics and Economic Growth. *National Bureau of Economic Research Working Paper*, 3668, March.

Barro, RJ (1991). Economic growth in a cross-section of countries. *Quarterly Journal of Economics*, 106, pp. 407–443.

Barro, RJ and X Sala-I-Martin (1992). Convergence. *Journal of Political Economy*, 100, pp. 223–251.

Bhagwati, J (2004). *In Defense of Globalization.* USA: Oxford University Press.

The Boston Consulting Group Report (2006). *The New Global Challengers: How 100 Top Companies from Rapidly Developing Economies Are Changing the World.*

The Boston Consulting Group Report (2005). *Navigating the Five Currents of Globalization: How Leading Companies Are Capturing Global Advantage.*

Bourguignon, F and C Morrisson (1999). *The Size Distribution of Income Among World Citizens: 1980–1990.* Mimeo, World Bank.

Collier, P (2007). *The Bottom Billion: Why the Poorest Countries are Failing and What Can Be Done About It.* USA: Oxford University Press.

Dollar, D and A Kraay (2001a). Trade, Growth, and Poverty. The World Bank, Development Research Group, Washington DC.

Dollar, D and A Kraay (2001b). Growth is Good for the Poor. The World Bank, Development Research Group, Washington DC.

Esteban, J and D Ray (1994). On the measurement of polarization. *Econometrica*, 62(4), pp. 819–851.

Foster, JE and M Wolfson (1992). Polarization and the decline of the middle class: Canada and the U.S. Mimeo, Vanderbilt University, Dep. of Economics.

Friedman, T (2005). *The World is Flat: A Brief History of the Twenty-First Century*, 1st Ed. Farrar, Straus and Giroux.

Heston, A, R Summers and A Bettina (2006). Penn World Table Version 6.2, Center for International Comparisons of Production, Income and Prices at the University of Pennsylvania.

Heston, A and R Summers (1991). The Penn World Table (Mark 5): An expanded set of international comparisons, 1950–1988. *Quarterly Journal of Economics*, 106(2), 327–368.

International Monetary Fund (2007). World Economic Outlook, Globalization and Inequality. Washington D.C: International Monetary Fund.

Lindert, PH and JG Williamson (2001). Does globalization make the world more unequal? *National Bureau of Economic Research Working Paper*, 8228, April.

Mankiw, NG, D Romer and DN Weil (1992). A contribution to the empirics of economic growth. *Quarterly Journal of Economics*, 107, pp. 407–437.

O'Rourke, KH (2001). Globalization and inequality: Historical trends. *National Bureau of Economic Research Working Paper*, 8339, June.

Persson, T and G Tabellini (1994). Is inequality harmful for growth? *American Economic Review*, 84(3), pp. 600–621.

Quah, DT (1996). Twin peaks: Growth and convergence in models of distribution dynamics. *The Economic Journal*, 106, pp. 1045–1055.

Ravallion, M (2001). Growth, inequality, and poverty: Looking beyond averages. *World Development*, 29(11), pp. 1803–1815.

Sachs, J (2006). *The End of Poverty: Economic Possibilities for Our Time*. New York: Penguin (Non-Classics).

Seshanna, S and S Decornez (2003). Income polarization and inequality across countries: An empirical study. *Journal of Policy Modeling*, 25(4).

Stiglitz, JE (2003). *Globalization and its Discontents*, 1st Ed. New York: WW Norton & Company.

Stiglitz, JE (2007). *Making Globalization Work*. WW Norton & Company.

Wolfson, MC (1994). When inequalities diverge. *American Economic Review*, 84(2), pp. 353–358.

Wolfson, MC (1997). Divergent inequalities: Theory and empirical results. *Review of Income and Wealth*, 43(4), pp. 401–421.

World Bank (2007). *World Development Indicators*. Washington, DC: World Bank.

Part III

Other Economic Issues

Chapter

10

Economics and Health

David Reisman

Everyone wants good health. There is no disagreement about that. Good health is consumption; people feel satisfied when they can climb stairs unaided and do not suffer polio because they have had the vaccine. Good health is investment; a student dreads a cold on the morning of an exam and a taxi driver loses business when he is laid up with emphysema. Good health is an end. Good health is a means. Good health is something that all people want.

The World Health Organization (WHO) defines good health as "a state of complete physical, mental and social well-being, and not merely the absence of disease". The road to the padded cell is paved with uncompromising completeness like this. It is healthy to have a little of what you fancy even if what makes you happy is fatty *char kway teow* (a local Singaporean dish). It is healthy to feel a bit low when you learn that you have been passed over for promotion again. It is healthy to feel exploited if the truth is that the boss is pushing too hard for his top-dollar bottom line. Too much completeness is bad for your health. Yet the WHO is on the right track. We all want to be free of crippling disease. We all want to live without unmanageable anxiety. We all want to turn up for work often enough to get our bonuses and our commissions. The philosophers try to put a name to the intuition. The rest of us simply sense that we know what good health is. We know what it is. We know that we like it. We know that we would like to have even more.

The doctor has sworn a Hippocratic oath to help a named, unique sick person without counting the cost. Yet the cost is there and the resources are scarce. It is the sad but necessary task of the economist to remind the community that there will never be enough to go round. One person's kidney transplant is another person's wonder-drug foregone. A budget plunged into hospitals is the same budget not ploughed into schools. Choices must be made. Economics makes a socially-useful contribution to the debate about health outcomes and medical inputs precisely because it helps the community to maximize the quantum of good health that can be squeezed from a given endowment that will never be enough.

Economics must rank the treatments and the options in terms of three criteria: (1) effectiveness: there is no point in backing a procedure if it does not restore the patient's function or if a do-nothing basepoint would, medically speaking, perform just as well. (2) efficiency: costs must be compared with benefits, private and social returns computed, an outside discounting-rate brought in, to establish if research on the cervix has as high an economic payoff as research on the prostate. (3) equity: the social value of fairness suggests that all citizens and residents should have equal access (assuming a reasonable capacity to benefit) to a basic package of decent-quality medical services. All health care redistributes. The sick consume more than the well. The old consume more than the young. Equity as an objective means that the State on behalf of the community shifts resources from the effective demand of the prosperous to the unmet needs of the distressed, the impoverished and the left-behind.

Economics makes a useful contribution where it helps the community to make rational choices and to assign non-random priorities. It also helps the community to understand the social function of pricing as a deterrent to over-consumption and a way of containing total cost. Fees and thresholds, forcing even clients with insurance to cover a part of the burden out of pocket or out of savings, make consumers think carefully about the extra anticipated improvement relative to the marginal payment that guards the gate. The downward-sloping demand curve is a people-centered relationship which gives ordinary individuals the freedom to quantify their subjective perceptions by indicating when they have had enough.

Cost-shares in an insured service, like free market prices in the supplying and demanding of wheat, at least empower the consumers to reveal their preferences through the pecuniary sacrifice that they make to satisfy each of their disparate wants. Payments also pick up both the price-elasticity and the income-elasticity of demand. Consumers move to the right along a demand curve when the price of a necessary but not an essential intervention drops. The whole demand curve shifts outwards to the right when rising incomes bring discretionary procedures within the choice set, when the price of a substitute (drugs versus surgeons) goes up, when the price of a complement (doctors matched up with beds) goes down.

The demand curve is pure psychology. The desire for care is a derived demand. It shadows the desire for a good health status that the payment is expected to bring into being. Patients cannot always put into words just how much they are willing to sacrifice. While questionnaires and surveys undoubtedly elicit valuable hypothetical information, data collected from a real-world demand curve is the best window the policy-maker will usually have into the contents of the invisible mind.

Rational people make rational choices. They proportion the extra benefit to the extra cost for all the consumables from which they wish to select a utility-maximizing portfolio mix. The equilibrium in that way becomes general and not merely partial. Yet there is a problem. In the market for apples, the shoppers have acquired knowledge through past purchases and the university of experience. In the market for disease and malfunction they are normally in the dark. Economics uses the concept of the agency relationship to model the contract between the ill-informed patient and the well-trained professional to whom he turns for diagnosis, advice and treatment.

The professional has an ethic of selfless service. He is a member of a professional body which stigmatises any abuse of information asymmetry. The professional is also, on the other hand, an economic human being who can be desperate for money to send his children to university or to buy his mother a retirement home of her own. Supplier-induced demand is the waste of resources that can so easily be the result where the professional demands marginal tests and unnecessary surgery exclusively because economics teaches that financial incentives produce the most economical use of scarce resources.

Incentives can be perverse where the doctor is paid a fee for his service and the patient hasn't a clue what he needs. Even so, the institutional structure can and does generate its own countervailing power. The general practitioner is charged with referrals to a surgeon who cannot therefore have things his own way. Besides that, the delivery of healthcare is often reimbursed by an insurance company or fund. Third-party payment restricts and rations in line with second opinions, preannounced criteria and prepublished scales. First-dollar coverage does not mean that the entitlement is infinite. Health insurance is in that sense the economist's best friend.

Healthcare, unlike most economic consumables, is frequently covered by prepayment through health insurance. Here again, the economist is able to provide a logical explanation for a typical economic phenomenon. From the perspective of the consumer, the reason is uncertainty. Fearing an unexpected catastrophe that he hopes will never occur, the risk-averter agrees to a small loss upfront in order to protect himself against a far greater loss when the veil of ignorance is finally lifted later on. From the insurer's point of view the reason is risk. The law of large numbers allows the speculator to make an informed guess as to the probable claims that will be made and to set an appropriate premium in the light of his most likely drains. Allowance must be made for the deadweight loading of marketing, administration and (for a commercial insurer) profits. Insurance is an unusual market. Policyholders, as a group, always take out less than what they put in.

Different premiums mean different volumes of business. Where oligopolists are struggling for market share, the logic of imperfect competition suggests that each insurer will target the low-risk, low-premium sector of the sales potential. Each will turn down known diabetics and haemophiliacs because they have a chronic condition. Each will specialize in services like paediatrics because a reputation for babies will not pull in the loss-making old. As the pool becomes larger, so the premiums will go up, it must happen as higher-risk consumers admitted into the club. The danger is that the good risks will react calculatively by dropping out altogether from the collective. They will opt to self-insure through personal savings. They will not want to be burdened with cross-subsidies for the smokers and the drinkers through premiums that are actuarially unfair to sensible people who always buckle their seat belt, eat two apples a day and go for a therapeutic jog.

The phenomenon is known as adverse selection. Where the good risks drop out and the bad risks cannot afford the higher premiums that result, the danger is that private insurance might effectively wither away. The alternative to nothing at all might have to be social insurance and single-pooled statism. Membership would be universal; to be a citizen is to be a paid-up part of the fund. Finance, from the employer and the employee, could be topped up out of tax (not least progressive income tax) as an expression of national solidarity. In some cases (as in the British National Health Service) the social insurance mechanism would be so closely entwined with the healthcare delivery mechanism that the organization that pays is effectively the organization that provides. Whatever the precise arrangements that are selected, the core legitimation is economic pragmatism. The commercial alternative fails to meet people's reasonable expectations. Market failure means that there is no insurer other than the State that can be trusted to take on the job.

The task of risk-rating the premiums is made more complicated by virtue of moral hazard. People who have bought insurance have less of an incentive to substitute prevention for cure. The contingencies being pooled, the calculative consumer has more of an incentive to play the free rider on the good health of others than he did before the insurance itself altered his risk profile for the worse. The insurer must not only predict the risk at entry but must predict the changes in the risk that the policy itself will gender. Insurers (aware as they must be of economic self-interest and the incentive to conceal the truth) can ask for information about pre-existent complaints, family history and life style. What no medical examination or DNA sample can ever pick up is, however, what the individual will be like in the future once prepaid access to doctoring has removed his economic incentive to look both ways before crossing the road or to check the date-stamp carefully before purchasing a fowl.

Economics is about allocative efficiency. It is also about innovation and change. Optimality can be dynamic as well as static. Thus the economist might recommend more medical schools and licensing bodies in order to foster monopolistic competition in place of suffocating monopoly that standardizes the hours and fixes the price. The economist might look to entrepreneurship for experimentation and novelty since it is competition that forces the incumbents and the entrants to differentiate and discount. The economist might be in favor of expensive scanners shared between several hospitals in order to maximize the economies of throughput and scale. The economist might be an advocate of replacement migration since capital must be complemented by labor and the market for auxiliaries, cleaners, nurses and doctors is often perilously tight.

And the economist must be in favor of the State. Regulations are needed to protect the patient from charlatan butchers and untrialled pharmaceuticals. Health education promotes nutritious pulses that make an investment in long-lived health capital. Pigovian taxes make cigarettes so costly that the impressionable young never catch the addiction. Targeted subsidies mean that hospitals will be situated in distant and underprivileged areas. Compulsory accounts like Medisave in Singapore mean that citizens must build up hypothecated balances against the chance of a future hospital bill. Environmental policies mean that agricultural land will be less polluted by pesticides and unleaded petrol will protect the lungs against toxic fumes. A top-notch infrastructure of road and reservoirs will keep the vegetables fresh and the drinking water clean. Good health is more than the doctors and the hospitals. It is also the internalization of the externalities that are a public good or a public bad for all.

Epidemics must be stemmed. Humanitarian values must be upheld. The market has no economic interest in supplying spillovers, non-excludable and non-rivalrous, which it cannot sell. Only the State can see to it that there is as much and as good for all.

The coordination must be done on a one-world basis. Haze, AIDS, contagious flu, contaminated beef, dangerous hallucinogens, the disposal of nuclear waste, global warming caused by the endangered ozone layer have consequences that extend beyond the national boundaries. Good health is a regional and a world-wide concern.

Yet good interventionism like good health costs money. Since the capacity to tax is not unlimited and since a budget deficit can cause destabilizing inflation, what is clear is that there is a strong case for growth. Rising productivity is rewarded with rising wages. Rising wages make possible better housing and nutritious food, more saving for a rainy day and buoyant sales taxes for the State to spend on immunization campaigns that make the rate of growth even more robust than before. Growth is not an unmixed blessing. Richer countries report more obesity and more stress. Yet growth is nonetheless the *sine qua non*. People want good health. People want rising standards of living. The two objectives are symbiotic, two sides of a single coin. Economy is in the enviable position of helping ordinary people to have more not just of one but of two good things that they want.

FURTHER READING

Morris, S, N Devlin and D Parkin (2007). *Economic Analysis in Health Care*. Chichester: Wiley.

Reisman, DA (2007). *Health Care and Public Policy*. Cheltenham: Elgar.

Santerre, RE and SP Neun (2007). *Health Economics: Theories, Insights and Industry Studies*. Mason: Thomson.

Chapter

11

Medical Decisions: A Two Stage Decision Model With Information Updating

*John Lane and Sandro Tsang**

INTRODUCTION

For many years now there has been widespread concern about the possible overuse of antibiotics in medical prescriptions. The World Health Organization (1999) has stated that the implied increase in antimicrobial resistance is a natural biological phenomenon amplified many-fold owing to human misuse and neglect. For example, in the UK, there is a significant risk that a stay in hospital may lead the patient to contract Clostridium Difficile or Methicillin resistant Staphylococcus aureus (MRSA), a bacterium which is resistant to a large group of antibiotics known as beta-lactarins (and which includes the

* We wish to pay tribute, and acknowledge our indebtedness, to the late Professor John Henry (of St Mary's Hospital in London and also Imperial College, London University) with whom we had many fruitful discussions on this topic and related matters. Our appreciation is also extended to Dr Xuelin Liu of the Asian Development Bank.

penicilins). For the latter condition, the overuse of antibiotics accentuates risk by eliminating useful microbes hence making its eradication very difficult.

Past attempts to search for an explanation have not been successful so we will consider only one such attempt, rather than providing a complete review of the literature. Ellis and McGuire (1986) presented a model in which the patient's medical condition is known and the patient is passive in that, he accepts as much treatment as the physician deems fit to supply. Basic economic principles tell us that the actual supply should be such that the benefit to the patient derived from the last unit of treatment is set equal to the incremental cost. In the jargon of economists the supplied quantity is such that the marginal benefit and marginal cost of treatment are equated. These marginal costs are typically presumed to be constant in the sense that they are independent of the quantity of treatment. On the other hand marginal benefit surely decreases when supplied quantity increases and, whilst one knows that for small treatment levels this marginal benefit is positive, excessive treatment levels will provide a negative marginal benefit (the treatment level for which the marginal benefit is zero will be referred to as the satiation level). When your physician prescribes antibiotics it is typically for a limited five day course of treatment for just such a reason.

The implication of this analysis is now clear. If marginal costs are positive then the supplied quantity will be less than the satiation level i.e. the level of treatment that the patient would prefer. Therefore there is an undersupply. This model can explain the overuse of antibiotics only if the treatment is sufficiently subsidized to ensure that the marginal cost to the physician is negative.

The above issue however, whilst relevant, is not paramount. The possible role of uncertainty in medical decision-making, first brought to our attention in an economic context by the renowned economist Arrow (1963), must be considered.

The malfeasance principle, the central tenet of "precautionary" decision-making, precludes an action being taken if it may cause unnecessary harm. However the physician has a duty to act even when confronted with uncertainty in the costs and benefits of treatment and also in the accuracy of the diagnosis. An evidence based decision-making process requires the physician to consider all the issues in making a balanced judgment, e.g. the likelihood of an incorrect diagnosis, or "false positive", can be reduced by increasing the quality of medical care but the resulting benefit must be evaluated relative to the increased costs.

This latter consideration is of increasing and extreme importance, now that the supply of new treatments is so dependent on expensive advanced technology and long lead-times in research and development. We have presumed in this discussion that the patient is passive which implies that his/her costs are covered either by a publicly funded National Health System, as in the UK, or by full-cover private health insurance. However there are many new treatments which are only on offer to the patient if treated privately because the National Institute of Health and Clinical Excellence, the UK Government's regulatory authority, has not approved its provision to the National Health Service. The decision is based on considerations of cost effectiveness. To give one such example, chosen from a long list, consider "wet age-related macular degeneration". This is a condition which causes blindness within three months if not treated. It can be treated with the drugs Lucentis or Macugen but this has only received a limited sanction for its provision by the UK's national Health System; one needs first to be blind in one eye and not too blind in the other.

In this Chapter, we consider a generic model which applies to a wide range of medical treatments; not solely that of antibiotic medication. We consider the effect of two sources of uncertainty in the decision-making process of a physician. In contrast to the Ellis and McGuire paper, we no longer assume that the patient's medical condition is known with certainty. The condition may be, for example, a benign form of cancer or an aggressive form of cancer. These conditions will be labeled X and Y respectively.

Alternatively one could be testing for the SARS virus (Y) against a common form of influenza (X), for Dengue fever (Y) or the Chikungunya virus, both of which are carried by the Aedes mosquito, against Malaria (X). Condition Y is deemed to be more serious than condition X in the sense that, for any given level of treatment, e.g. radiotherapy and/or chemotherapy for cancer, the incremental benefit to the patient is larger if he has condition Y rather than the alternative condition X. This implies that the satiation level of treatment for condition Y exceeds that of condition X.

The initial (or *a priori*) information available to the physician is limited to the knowledge of the proportion of the population at large that has condition Y. However, when first meeting a particular and random patient drawn from this population, this information by itself is not sufficient for the choice of an appropriate treatment. It is necessary to perform a diagnostic test, the result of which could be the prediction that the cancer is benign (diagnosis x) or aggressive (diagnosis y). Thus, diagnosis y is the prediction that the true medical condition of the patient, equivalently the patient's "type", is Y; similarly x predicts X. This information is then used to update the physician's initial or *a priori* estimates of the likelihood that the patient has condition Y (alternatively X). These updated (or "posterior") probabilities are obtained in accordance with a well known theorem in statistics, namely Bayes' theorem, which will be discussed in Section 1 of this Chapter.

The second source of uncertainty is that, very few diagnostic tests are infallible. It is possible that a patient's diagnostic result is y, even though the true condition is X. This is referred to as a "false positive". For example, it has been estimated that 10% of mammogram tests for breast cancer yield false positives; the unfortunate patient is treated for this condition even though there is no problem.

The final consideration that we wish to introduce into our reasoning is to allow the physician to choose between a range of possible diagnostic tests of different quality. Higher quality indicates that the likelihood of a false positive, decreases. The posterior probabilities referred to above will now be contingent on, or functions of, the chosen quality level. This increase in quality will mean higher costs of provision but also increased benefits to the patient.

Therefore, there are three decision variables and they must be chosen to maximize a weighted average of the benefit to the patient and the profits of the physician. The weights reflect the physician's degree of altruism towards the patient. Perfect altruism indicates the absence of any financial concern. Also the benefit to the patient is stochastic (uncertain). Therefore, in accordance with standard procedures for decision making under uncertainty, it is taken to be a weighted average of the benefit of treatment to the patient if he is type X and also that if he is type Y. The weights are given by the physician's updated beliefs, after diagnosis, of the patient's type.

The mathematical complexity of this decision process suggests that one adopts a "two stage" optimization procedure. One first determines the diagnostic contingent treatment levels for any given level of quality, or any given diagnostic test. These are called treatment functions. After substitution of the treatment functions into the physician's objective function there will be only one variable, namely quality, over which the maximization proceeds. The optimizing quality level is then substituted into the treatment functions to determine the quantity of medical services which should be provided. The first stage of this "two stage" procedure is discussed in Section 2, the second stage in Section 3 and further results and conclusions are discussed in Section 4.

1. INFORMATION UPDATING

To comprehend how the physician's prior beliefs should be modified after knowing the result of the diagnostic test, i.e. to understand the Bayesian updating procedure, consider the following example which is based on realistic data. Let's suppose that all women aged 40 (the "population") participate in routine screening for breast cancer and 1% of them have breast cancer. Then the prior probability of medical condition Y is $P(Y) = 0.01$ and of the alternative condition (no breast cancer) is $P(X) = 0.99$. It is known that 80% of women with breast cancer will get positive (y) mammographies (the diagnostic test). Thus, in an obvious notation, $P(y/Y)$ is 0.80. Also the probability that the diagnosis is positive even though the patient does not have breast cancer is 9.6% so $P(y/X) = 0.096$ i.e. a "false positive", a positive but incorrect diagnosis. The question is: if a woman in this age group had a positive mammography in routine screening what is the probability that she actually has breast cancer?

Surveys have shown that an overwhelming majority of General Practitioner doctors (commonly referred to as GP's in the UK) will answer 80% i.e. P(y/Y). If the patient was you, then you would have cause to panic. In fact we are being asked for P(Y/y), the probability that the patient's true medical condition is that of cancer given that the patient has had a positive diagnosis. These two magnitudes can be very different and their causal relationship with each other is given by Bayes' Theorem.

What is needed is an estimate of this probability for a particular and random patient drawn from this population but, the above data is aggregative in nature. To proceed note that P(Y/y) is the same as the probability that the medical condition is Y given that we restrict out attention to the subset of the population who receive a positive diagnosis, in other words, diagnosis y occurs with certainty. Let P(y) be the proportion of the total population that will receive a positive diagnosis and note that the random variables Z = X,Y and z = x,y are independently distributed. Therefore the probability of having condition Y, within the whole population and not just the above subset, is obtained by multiplication of the two terms: P(Y/y) P(y). However this is the same as P(y/Y) P(Y) because in both cases the patient has both condition Y and diagnosis y. Therefore:

$$P(Y/y) = P(y/Y)\ P(Y)/P(y).$$

Also note that P(y), by a similar argument to that used above, is given by:

$$P(y/Y)\ P(Y) + P(y/X)\ P(X).$$

The first term is the likelihood of having a positive and true diagnosis, the second a positive but false diagnosis. These two equations together are the constituent parts of Bayes' Theorem so with a little algebra one can write:

$$P(Y/y) = 1/\{1 + [P(X)/P(Y)]/L\} \qquad \text{where } L = P(y/Y)/P(y/X).$$

L is called the likelihood ratio. It is the probability of a true positive divided by the probability of a false positive. In our example, by direct substitution, $1/L = 12\%$ and $P(X)/P(Y) = 99$ so $P(Y/y) = 7.8\%$.

In contrast to the earlier and common miss-interpretation of the data, the patient indeed has a reason to be concerned, but perhaps there is no reason to panic just yet. A reduction from 80% to just 7.8% is rather significant.

Now let us suppose that the physician can select from a wide variety of diagnostic tests and think of each one being in a one to one correspondence with quality q. Then the quality variable q determines the value of L, $L = L(q)$ say. An increase in quality would increase the likelihood ratio L so the posterior probability $P(Y/y)$ of the diagnostic result being a correct predictor increases. It becomes 1, if the test is infallible. Conversely if it decreases then the posterior probability decreases and could become zero.

Therefore there must be a critical level of quality, Q say, with the property that the posterior likelihood $P(Y/y)$ exceeds the prior likelihood $P(Y)$ if, and only if, the physician selects a quality in excess of Q. Furthermore it is easy to show that $P(X/x)$ exceeds $P(X)$ if and only if q exceeds the same critical value Q. This critical quality level satisfies $L(q) = 1$; the probabilities of a true positive and a false positive are equal.

One would like the results of the diagnostic test to be more accurate predictors of the patient's medical condition than the prior probabilities. Whether or not the parameters of the model (such as the remuneration structure, the marginal benefit functions and the physician's degree of altruism) have the property that, the physician's selected quality level exceeds Q, is a matter to be discussed in Section 3.

2. DIAGNOSTIC CONTINGENT TREATMENTS

We now consider the relationship between treatment levels and quality levels if the diagnosis is positive (y) and also if the diagnosis is negative (x). In Lane and Tsang (2008) it was shown that these relationships are identical if the independent variable is P(y/X) in the former case, but P(x/X) in the latter and also the marginal cost of treatment is independent of the diagnosis. Note that these probabilities are determined by the quality level but, in accordance with our intuition, whilst P(y/X) decreases with increasing quality, P(x/X) increases. The implication can then be shown that if the diagnosis is y, then the supplied quantity of medical treatment must increase with quality i.e., these two commodities are complementary. In contrast, if the diagnosis is x, then quantity must decrease with increasing quality i.e., the two commodities are substitutable. The increase in quality has an asymmetric impact on treatment levels.

It can further be shown that these two treatment levels are independent of the diagnosis only if quality q is set at its critical level Q. There is then no purpose in spending money on a diagnostic test if the chosen quality of the test is Q or something less than this. Nonetheless, with an inappropriate remuneration structure, this may happen.

The final result is that the treatment quantity for the more serious medical condition exceeds that of the alternative if and only if, the chosen quality level exceeds its critical value.

The reader should now be able to draw the graph (against quality) of these two diagnostic contingent treatment functions, on the basis of the information given above. Now call the satiation level of treatment for the x-condition T(x) and that for the y-condition T(y), where T(y) exceeds T(x). The patient would like to be supplied in accordance with these satiation levels. But it would be fortuitous indeed if these two targets could be achieved, or implemented, on the basis of just one choice of quality level. This is a general principle in economics. We return to this issue in Section 4.

3. DIAGNOSTIC QUALITY

Analytically, one must substitute the treatment functions derived above into the objective function of the physician. There is then just one independent variable, namely quality, and in principle, it is clear that the best choice is that the incremental "cost" of an additional unit of quality is equal to the additional "benefit". Parentheses have been used to emphasise that these terms include both direct and indirect effects and so are quite complex to evaluate. For example, the incremental cost is not simply the extra direct cost of quality provision but must also include its effect on differential treatment levels, weighted by the altruism parameter and the sensitivity of P(x) with respect to quality.

What can be shown is that, under quite reasonable assumptions, the incremental cost is positive. On the other hand the incremental benefit, whilst positive if q exceeds Q, may otherwise be positive or negative. In the latter case the best choice of quality exceeds its critical level. In the former case, with the "wrong" remuneration structure and/or a sufficient absence of altruism, the choice may be below its critical level even though this leads to the use of posterior predictions which are worse than those given by the prior probabilities.

If there is an increase in altruism this best choice of quality will also increase. Better communication between physicians and patients, or the persuasive power of demanding patients, could be thought of as equivalent to an increase in altruism. Also, if the prior probability of a random patient being type Y should decrease, then quality will increase i.e., if it is less likely that a random patient is Y-type then greater care or quality provision is necessary in order to correctly identify them.

Finally, note that substitution of this quality choice, into the treatment functions, provides the diagnostic contingent treatment levels.

4. IMPLICATIONS AND CONCLUSIONS

It helps to have some notation. Let b(X) and b(Y) be the type-contingent marginal benefit functions where the independent variable, treatment quantity, has been subsumed. Let b(x) and b(y) be the diagnostic contingent (expected) marginal benefit functions. Because they are weighted averages (with weights summing to one) of the type-contingent marginal benefit functions, they are both greater than b(X) and smaller than b(Y), for any given level of treatment. Furthermore, if the chosen quality level exceeds its critical value Q, then we can order these marginal benefit functions as below:

$$b(X) \leq b(x) \leq b(y) \leq b(Y) \qquad \text{for any given level of treatment.}$$

The diagnostic contingent marginal benefit functions will lie closer to their respective type-contingent marginal benefit functions if the quality of the diagnostic test is increased. This has the effect of reducing the biases in treatment discussed below.

The ordering of b(x) and b(y) would be reversed if the chosen quality level was less than Q.

Let us suppose that the remuneration structure is such that the physician chooses q larger than Q. Then the above ordering implies that if the marginal "cost" of treatment is zero, as under a full cost reimbursement scheme, then the patient with the less serious medical condition X will be oversupplied; actual supply exceeds T(X), the satiation level for this type. Similarly the seriously ill patient with medical condition Y, will be undersupplied.

This provides a possible explanation for the overuse of antibiotics. It does not, however, imply that the physician is irrational. On the contrary, the physician must be cogniscent of the possibility that the patient with an x diagnosis, who will therefore be treated as an X-type patient, may in fact be Y-type and vice-versa. There is an implicit insurance aspect within this decision making process.

If we now consider any type of partial reimbursement scheme, then the implied constant and positive level of marginal costs, if not "too large", induces a reduction in the oversupply to the patient with a negative diagnosis, then the problem is mitigated. However if the diagnosis is positive there will be an increase in the degree of undersupply.

If there was no diagnostic test, so the patient is to be treated in an identical fashion irrespective of his true condition, the (expected) marginal benefit function would lie between the two diagnostic marginal benefit functions. This leads to an increase in the above biases. The diagnostic test mitigates these biases but does not fully eliminate them.

Also observe that if the ordering of the diagnostic contingent marginal benefit functions is reversed, then the above results remain valid but the biases will be more extreme.

The fundamental difficulty is that the pricing structure in all of the above cases is inappropriate. As mentioned earlier, if the patient trusts that the diagnosis is accurate, he will wish to be supplied in accordance with his satiation levels T(X) and T(Y). There are two target values, but there is only one control namely, quality.

However we have assumed that the marginal cost of treatment quantities is independent of the diagnosis. If we allow for differential pricing based on the actual diagnosis then we will have introduced one more control. It is then easy to show that if the treatment when the diagnosis is y, is subsidized, but when it is x, it is taxed, then there is a tax/subsidy system for which the induced choice of quality will generate the required satiation treatment levels.

END NOTES

Arrow, KJ (1963). Uncertainty and the welfare economics of medical care. *American Economic Review* 53, pp. 941-973.

Ellis, RP and TG McGuire (1986). Provider of behaviour under prospective reimbursement: Cost sharing and supply. *Journal of Health Economics*, 5, pp. 129-152.

Lane, J and S Tsang (2008). Uncertainty in the economics of medical decisions. *Singapore Economic Review*, 53(1), pp. 81-101.

World Health Organization (WHO) (1999). Containing Antimicrobial Resistance, Review of the literature and report of WHO workshop on the development of a global strategy for the containment of anti-microbial resistance, Geneva, Switzerland. CDS/CSR/DRS.

Chapter

12

Economics of Love: A Simple Theory and Empirical Study in Singapore

Ho Kong Weng

Love is hard to measure as it has many dimensions and involves different people with different background and purposes or utility functions. Motivated by a passage from the Bible, we will focus on three dimensions of love in our simple economic framework of love from parents to children. The first dimension is related to time, namely, its everlasting nature. In our economic framework, the planning horizon is effectively infinite, incorporating children's concern into the optimization of parents. The second dimension is altruism, which is a care for others with sacrifice. Parents invest their time and money in the future of their children instead of enjoying consumption and leisure for themselves. These efforts by the parents are sacrifices, or costs of producing love for their children. Are there benefits of producing love for their children? The benefits could be tangible or intangible in the form of future support from their children in old age and returned love from their children. However, these future benefits rely on hopes or expectations which may not even materialize eventually. The final dimension of love in our model is a value system of rights and wrongs perceived by the parents and to be transmitted to their children. Without this value system, love will not rejoice with truth and what is produced may become hatred instead of love. Based on simple optimizations of parents and children, a demand-supply framework of love will be developed. Shifts in the demand and supply curves will be used to illustrate changes in the equilibrium of love. A simple empirical study on love among parents and their children will be presented, illustrating how love may be quantified in a simple manner.

INTRODUCTION

Standard simple economic models rely on a well functioning price mechanism to bring buyers and sellers of a good or service together in a market, whereby changes in the price of the good or service will lead to changes in the quantity demanded and the quantity supplied, until a market equilibrium is reached, meaning that both buyers and sellers are satisfied with the market clearing price at which the good or service is traded. The simplest setting leading to an equalization of quantity demanded and quantity supplied assumes that the good or service is identical regardless of quantity exchanged, both the buyers and sellers are homogenous price takers solving their selfish well-being maximization problems, and, more fundamentally, the market exists with an observable price for a measurable good or service.

Different from many economic goods and services with well-defined markets of exchange, love among people has many dimensions, is hard to be quantified, and involves people with different background and purposes or utility functions. In particular, is there a market for love? What is the price of love?

In the prostitution market of temporary love, the price of so called love is observable and measurable but its associated but hidden price of potential HIV transmission and impact on families could be less observable and under-measured. In the marriage market of more lasting love, men and women are both buyers and sellers. The price of a marriage may be related to the amount of dowry, the expenditure of a wedding banquet, cost of dates and gifts given before marriage, and cost of time in knowing one another as the Ms. Right, or Mr. Right. However, the price of marriage love is perceived with uncertainty about the future. "Married happily ever after" may not be the norm as we observe a rising divorce rate in Singapore and many other countries. Since not all of us have participated in the above-mentioned markets of love, this Chapter will focus on the market of love among parents and children in which all of us have first-hand experience either as a parent or as a child.

In the development of an economic model of love among parents and their children, we find it helpful to examine the characteristics of love as documented by non-economists. E.g., 1 Corithians 13: 4-8a of the English Standard Version of the Bible reads,

> "*Love is patient and kind; love does not envy or boast; it is not arrogant or rude. It does not insist on its own way; it is not irritable or resentful; it does not rejoice at wrongdoing, but rejoices with the truth. Love bears all things, believes all things, hopes all things, endures all things. Love never ends*".

The above passage suggests three important dimensions of love which we will take into consideration in the exploration of a simple economic framework of love transmitted from parents to children. The first dimension is related to time, namely, its everlasting nature. In the simple economic framework, the planning horizon is effectively infinite, incorporating children's concern into the optimization of parents. The second dimension is altruism, which is a care for others with sacrifice. Parents invest their time and money in the future of their children instead of enjoying consumption and leisure for themselves. These efforts by the parents are sacrifices, or costs of producing love for their children. Are there benefits of producing love for their children? The benefits could be tangible or intangible in the form of future support from their children in old age and returned love from their children. However, these future benefits rely on hopes or expectations which may not even materialize eventually. The final dimension of love in our model is a value system of rights and wrongs perceived by the parents and to be transmitted to their children. Without this value system, love will not rejoice with truth and what is produced may become hatred instead of love. In summary, an economic framework of love with marginal benefits equated to marginal costs has to be based on a value system and an effectively infinite planning horizon. Based on the above simple optimization model of love, a demand and supply framework will be developed, showing a market equilibrium of love.

The remaining of the paper is as follows. Section 1 will develop a simple mathematical model of parental love, and derive the supply and demand curves of love. Section 2 will examine some theoretical implications of the model. Section 3 will present a simple empirical study on love among parents and their children, illustrating how love may be quantified in a simple manner, followed by discussions on its main findings in Section 4. Section 5 will provide the concluding remarks.

1. A SIMPLE MATHEMATICAL MODEL OF PARENTAL LOVE

The three aspects of (parental) love identified earlier are namely: (1) it is everlasting, (2) it is sacrifice, and (3) it is concerned with right and wrong. For the first aspect on an infinite planning horizon, the optimization of a parent considers the welfare of its child and in turn, when the child becomes a parent, the welfare of its child, or the grandchild of the first parent will be considered. The intergenerational linkage is likened to an everlasting time horizon. The sacrificial nature of love is taken to be the parental cost involved in producing love for the child. In particular, assume that more time spent investing in the human capital of the child means less time for parental engagement of market activities and as a result less parental consumption. Furthermore, the parent's preference for investing in the "good" and "bad" stocks of human capital depends on the value system of the parent. In particular, assume that love is generated from the investment in the "good" stock of human capital but not from the "bad" stock of human capital.

The selfish child spends effort measured in time to gain parental attention and satisfaction derived from parental attention and in return he/she will take care of the parent in old age if he/she turns out to be a "good" son or daughter. A more happy childhood due to parental attention will translate to more care given by the "good" son or daughter to the parent in old age. The production of love among the parent and the child is a function of both the time spent by the parent investing in the "good" stock of human capital of the child and the time spent by the child in pleasing the parent and gaining happiness in childhood. The price of love is the probability that the son or daughter will turn out to be a "good" son or daughter loving and caring for his/her parent in old age. The model is simple and attempts to capture some important characteristics of parental love while assuming away other aspects which could be realistic but may be studied in further extensions of the basic model developed here.

1.1. Optimization of Parent and Supply of Love

The representative parent maximizes the following utility function by choosing the amount of time at work t_w, time in investing the "good" stock of human capital for the child t_h, and time in investing the "bad" stock of human capital t_k:

$$\max \quad \theta c_p^{1/2} + \beta\{pv_l h_c + (1-p)v_n k_c\},$$

$$\text{subject to} \quad h_c = t_h^{1/2},$$

$$k_c = t_k^{1/2},$$

$$t_w + t_h + t_k = 1,$$

$$c_p = t_w w_p,$$

where $\theta > 0$ is a parameter attached to parental consumption c_p, $0 < \beta < 1$ is the parental discount factor for the future, h_c is the "good" stock of human capital, k_c is the "bad" stock of human capital, p is the probability of the child turning "good", $v_l > 0$ is the value attached to "good" or the child "loving" the parent in old age, and $v_n > 0$ is the value attached to "bad" or the child "not loving" the parent in old age, and w_p is the wage rate received by the parent.

Based on the above optimization, we will be able to derive a positive relation between t_b and p. Since love rejoices with truth and what is good, it is natural to specify that the quantity of love L supplied by the parent is positively related to t_b, which is the time spent investing in the "good" stock of human capital. We take p, the probability of the child becoming a "good" child who loves and takes care of the parent in old age, to be the price of love. Hence, we will get a positive relation between L and p, which is the supply curve of love.

1.2. Optimization of Child and Demand of Love

The representative child maximizes the following utility function by choosing time spent in pleasing the parent t_p and time spent for himself/herself t_c:

$$\max \quad \phi t_p^{1/2} + \mu t_c^{1/2} + \gamma\{pU_l + (1-p)U_n\},$$

$$\text{subject to} \quad U_l = \frac{u_l b_c}{t_p^2},$$

$$U_n = u_n k_c,$$

$$t_p + t_c = 1,$$

where $\phi > 0$ is a parameter attached to satisfaction from parental attention, $\mu > 0$ is a parameter attached to independence or freedom, $0 < \gamma < 1$ is the child's discount factor for the future, U_l is the utility of the "good" child, $u_l > 0$ is a value attached to being "good" and "loving" the parent in old age, U_n is the utility of the "bad" child, and $u_n > 0$ is the value attached to being "bad" and "not loving" the parent in old age. Note that a higher t_p, which is time spent by the child pleasing and with the parent, will automatically translate into a lower utility of the "good" child as he or she will spend more resources, likely to be both money and time, on the parent, taking care of the parent and sacrificing his or her own welfare in adulthood. A higher t_p produces more guilt or a higher sense of obligation to take care of the parent in old age.

Based on the optimization of the child, we may derive a negative relation between t_p and p. Since love L is positively related to t_p, which is time spent by the child pleasing and with the parent, we will have a negative relation between L and p, which is price of love as argued earlier, or a demand curve of love.

1.3. Market Equilibrium of Love

Bringing the supply and demand curves of love together in the same diagram gives the market equilibrium of love, indicated by the intersection of the two curves. For simplicity, we have drawn two linear functions in Fig. 1. In general, they could be non-linear.

This is not the usual market of traditional goods and services but involves the optimizations of parents and children over time with

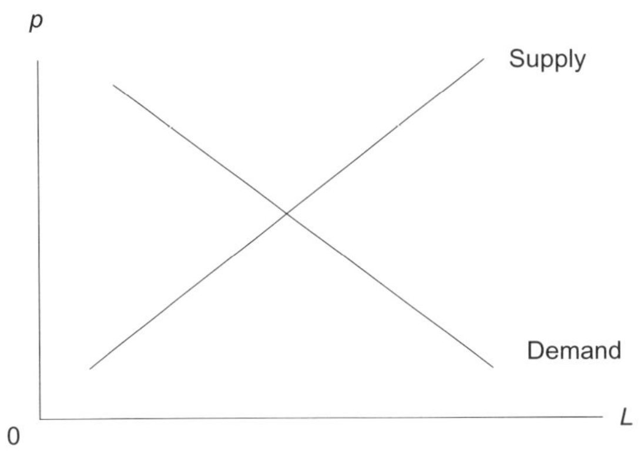

Figure 1. Market equilibrium of love

uncertainty, and the probability associated with the "good" state is taken to be the price of love, which is good in nature. Such a demand-supply framework enables us to analyze the impact on the equilibrium quantity of love and the price of love given changes in some exogenous parameters in the model.

2. THEORETICAL IMPLICATIONS

In this section, we will consider the theoretical predictions of the model given two changes: (1) an increase in the parental "morality", and (2) an increase in the quality of time spent with parents during childhood.

2.1. An Increase in Parental "Morality"

Consider an increase in v_l, the parental value attached to "good" or the child "loving" the parent in old age. This is likened to a shift in parental preference from "bad" to "good", and simply assumed to be an increase in parental "morality". As a consequence, the parent will produce more love (which is good) *via* spending more time in the "good" stock of human capital at all levels of price p. The supply curve will shift out to the right as depicted in Fig. 2.

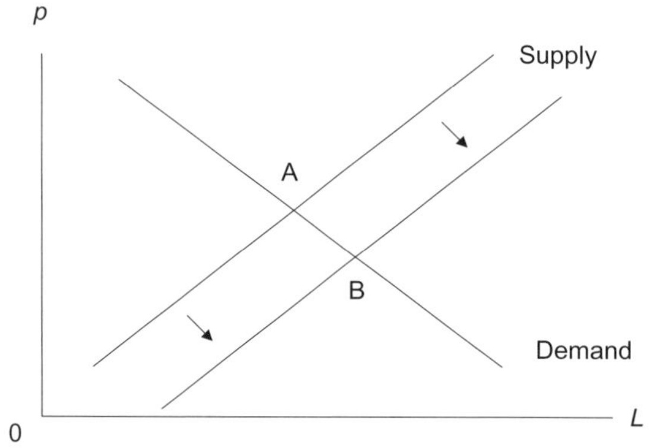

Figure 2. Increase in parental "morality"

Consequently, the equilibrium quantity of love is increased. However, the price of love is now lowered. The reason for a decrease in the price of love is a downward sloping demand curve of love: a higher quantity of love demanded is associated with a lower price of love. Since the price of love is also the probability of the child turning "good", we may be puzzled by why an increase in the parental "morality" will lead to a lower probability of the child turning "good". The child is selfish and also enjoys time for himself/herself; therefore, in order to induce him/her to have more time with the parent, who produces the increased love, the probability that he/she has to sacrifice in the future, taking care of the parent, must be lowered.

Another way to understand the theoretical result intuitively is to think of an expected level of equilibrium love pL. Suppose love L is only realized when the child turns "good" with a probability p. Hence pL is the expected love realized. While p has decreased, L has increased, with the product pL increased or decreased depending on the elasticity of the demand and supply curves. E.g., the decrease in p may be small while the increase in L may be large, resulting in an overall increase in pL. This is the case where the demand curve has a gentle slope and the supply curve has a steep slope.

2.2. An Increase in Quality of Time with Parents in Childhood

Consider an increase in ϕ, the degree of satisfaction from parental attention or interpreted as the extent of quality time with parents in childhood. The child will then spend more time with the parent, leading to an upward shift of the demand curve, and resulting in a higher equilibrium quantity of love and a higher price of love or a higher probability of the child turning "good". Figure 3 illustrates the impact on the market equilibrium of love.

In this situation, it is unambiguous that the expected equilibrium quantity of love, defined as pL, will increase as both L and p increase given an increase in the quality of time with parents in childhood.

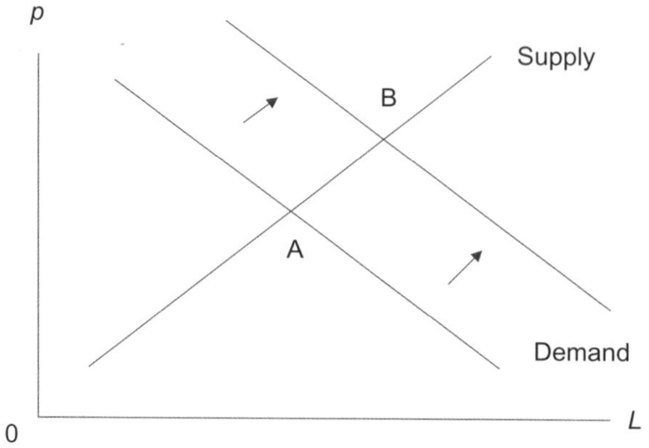

Figure 3. Increase in quality of time with parents in childhood

3. AN EMPIRICAL STUDY

An exploratory survey on quantifying love was conducted among students and their parents in 2007. Five schools participated in this project and classes were randomly selected from the complete lists of classes in each school. The survey forms were then given to students in the selected classes. A total of 2500 forms were distributed and 624 students returned the forms, giving a response rate of about 25%. As the project is basically unfunded without incentive for interviewees, the attained response rate is encouraging to us.

The average age of the student sample is 15.2 years, with 30.5% males and 69.5% females as 2 of the schools involved are girl schools. 89.6% are Singaporeans, and 95.9% are Chinese. Respondents are asked to rank the importance of various aspects of love received from parents and to quantify on a scale from 1 to 100, the corresponding amount of love associated with these different dimensions of parental love: monetary or material provision for child, giving freedom to child, emotional support for child, moral values transmitted to child, and guiding child in terms of setting goals. There are questions on interactions among parents and their teenage children such as number of meals taken together, frequencies of doing things they like together and one-to-one talks, and whether there is enough communication between parents and children. The last question asks the students to rate the overall love on a scale from 1 to 100 received from their fathers and mothers.

Our approach of quantifying love is based on self-reported scores for love received from parents. This approach assumes true revelations of the respondents and that the respondents understand the meaning of the range of the scores given. As the respondents are students from the same educational system in Singapore, the love scale from 1 to 100 would suggest a similar scale for academic results in Singapore and they are likely to use a common reference in rating love received from their parents.

Table 1 shows the average scores for various aspects of and overall parental love received. Overall love from mothers seems to be slightly higher than overall love from fathers. Fathers score lower in emotional support for their children than mothers. The top scorer in paternal love is monetary or material provision; for maternal love, it is moral value transmission. Based on these summary statistics, we see a gender role of love transmission: fathers specialize in certain aspects of love while mothers specialize in others. We will discuss the gender role of love transmission further in the next section. Guidance in setting goals is the lowest aspect of love received among the five aspects of parental love.

Table 1: Average parental love received

Aspects of Love	Father	Mother
Monetary/Material Provision	74.2 (24.0)	73.3 (24.1)
Giving Freedom	73.4 (22.7)	70.1 (23.4)
Emotional Support	62.5 (28.3)	72.5 (24.2)
Moral Value Transmission	71.0 (25.4)	76.0 (22.3)
Guidance in Goal-Setting	59.4 (28.9)	62.9 (28.0)
Overall	79.2 (23.1)	84.8 (19.1)

Note: Figures in parentheses refer to standard deviation.

4. DISCUSSIONS

In this section, we will report results from simple regressions to show that love transmission is time intensive, fathers and mothers specialize in different aspects of love, and that moral values and emotional support are important determinants of love transmission.

4.1. Spend Time, Not Money, to Transmit Love

We regress the overall love from father or mother on number of meals taken together, frequency of doing things together, frequency of one-to-one talks, and whether there is enough communication between parents and children, with controls on age and gender of the students. Our results show that all these time-intensive activities explain the quantity of parental love received very well and are statistically significant at 5% level. We have added other money-related variables on the right-hand side of the regression but they are all insignificant in explaining parental love received. The message is, time but not money, is crucial in transmitting love.

4.2. Parental Gender Specialization in Love Transmission

Next, we regress the overall paternal love on the various aspects of paternal love to find out what aspects of love are important in explaining overall love received from fathers with controls on age and gender of the students. Likewise we perform the regression analysis on maternal love. The results are reported in Table 2. Monetary provision and emotional support from fathers are important determinants of paternal love. Although fathers on average do not score well on emotional support as reported in Table 1, those who do well, improves the paternal overall love transmitted significantly. The regression suggests that a one-point increase in the score of fatherly emotional support will increase overall love by 0.4 point. Older students tend to receive lower overall love from fathers, accordingly to our regression results. In contrast to love from fathers, the overall love

Table 2: Gender specialization of love transmission

Overall Love	Father	Mother
Monetary/Material Provision	0.11***	0.02
Giving Freedom	−0.00	0.02
Emotional Support	0.40***	0.27***
Moral Value Transmission	0.03	0.10**
Guidance in Goal-Setting	0.06	0.07**
Age	−0.96**	−0.17
Male	−0.05	−2.58*

Note: Constant term is not reported for simplicity. Coefficients with*,**, and *** are statistically significant at 10%, 5%, and 1% level, respectively.

from mothers is significantly explained by emotional support, moral value transmission, and guidance in goal setting. Mothers seem to be better in showing love *via* guidance in moral values and goal setting. Daughters seem to report more overall love received from mothers than sons. The results in Table 2 suggest that fathers and mothers have a division of labor in the transmission of love to their children. Since fathers are usually the bread winners or earn more than mothers in the formal labor market, they focus on monetary or material provision as a channel of love for their children while mothers focus on other aspects of love within the family such as moral value transmission, guidance in goal setting. Emotional support is an important channel of love transmission for both fathers and mothers.

4.3. Importance of Moral Value and Emotional Support

Table 3 reports the average ranking on various aspects of parental love as reported by the students. According to these average rankings, emotional support is the most important channel of love, and moral value transmission from parents is the second most important channel. Monetary or material provision is the least important channel among the five aspects of parental love.

When we run parental overall love regressions on the various rankings reported by the students, we find that rankings of emotional

Table 3: Student ranking on aspects of parental love

Aspects of Parental Love	Average Ranking
Monetary/Material Provision	4.0
Giving Freedom	2.9
Emotional Support	1.7
Moral Value Transmission	2.5
Guidance in Goal-Setting	3.7

Note: A smaller number means a higher rank or greater importance.

support, moral value transmission, and guidance in goal setting are statistically significant. As the ranking of these aspects of parental love improves, the overall love received will increase too.

5. CONCLUSION

Our empirical results suggest that the transmission of parental love is time intensive, fathers and mothers divide the task of transmitting love to their children according to their comparative advantages, and moral values and emotional support are important aspects of parental love for their children. These findings are supporting evidence for our theoretical model which focuses on the three aspects of love: love is sacrifice, love is about right and wrong and, love never ends.

Chapter

13

The Role of Exchange Rates in Foreign Direct Investment: A United States Perspective

Ho Woon Yee

International transactions of goods, service and assets determine a country's exchange rate but the exchange rate for seemingly good reasons does not influence the international purchases and sale of assets. If a foreign asset generates a future stream of profits denominated in foreign currency and if the profits will be converted back into the domestic currency at the same exchange rate, the present discounted value of the investment will not be affected by the level of the exchange rate. This chapter presents recent developments in the academic literature on FDI with specific references to Froot and Stein (1991) and Blonigen (1997). The studies show that when selected conditions under perfect markets are relaxed, exchange rates perform a definite role in explaining FDI flows. Under these conditions, the connection between real exchange rate levels and FDI become clearly unambiguous.

INTRODUCTION

In a world of capital mobility, a country's exchange rate is determined by balances in the capital and current accounts. The component investment flows within the capital account, particularly the relative magnitude of portfolio verses direct investments are not affected by changes in the exchange rates. Yet, the view that exchange rates play no role in affecting FDI flows is at odds with empirical observations that higher FDI flows into the United States is associated with lower values of the US dollar.[1] This chapter presents recent developments in the literature on foreign direct investment (FDI) that explains the influence of exchange rates on FDI inflows. The chapter proceeds with a review of exchange rate determination, followed by a discussion of foreign portfolio investment and direct investment. The discussion highlights the differences in motivations for portfolio and direct investment flows and then addresses the role of exchange rates in FDI inflows with specific references to Froot and Stein (1991) and Blonigen (1997). Both studies exemplify the complementary but varied approaches used to explain the causes of FDI flows.

DETERMINATION OF EXCHANGE RATES

International transactions make it necessary for the currency of a country to be traded for another. The rate at which two currencies are traded is known as the bilateral exchange rate. For example, if one US dollar can be exchanged for 110 Japanese yen, the exchange rate between the United States and Japanese currencies is 110 yen per dollar. In a flexible exchange rate regime, the value of a currency is determined by the supply and demand for the currency in the foreign exchange market, a market in which currencies of various nations are traded for one another.

In the foreign exchange market, the supply of dollars is the amount of dollars that the household and firms offer for trade with other currencies. It is not the same as the money supply set by the central bank. While the central bank determines the total supply of dollars in the economy, a dollar is not counted as having been supplied to the foreign exchange market until holders of dollars, such as

[1] Caves (1989) shows evidence of exchange rate correlation with FDI inflows.

a household or firm trade the dollar for a foreign currency. Similarly, the demand for dollars in the foreign exchange market is not the same as the domestic demand for money, but the number of dollars that holders of foreign currencies seek to buy.

In the case of the United States, the key suppliers of US dollars in the foreign exchange market are, US households and firms and they do so for two main reasons. Firstly, a US household or firm wants to purchase a foreign good or service. For example, an American household wants to buy a car made in Japan and supplies US dollars in the foreign exchange market for yen to import the Japanese car. Likewise, an American traveling to Japan requires yen to make purchases when he is in Osaka and supplies the US dollars for yen. Secondly, a US household or firm wants to purchase a foreign asset. With savings, a US household could purchase stocks issued by firms in Japan. Because the stocks from Japan are priced in yen, the US household or firm will supply US dollars for yen to acquire Japanese assets. The supply of US dollars to the foreign exchange market is shown by the upward sloping curve in Fig. 1. While we focus on the market in which US dollars are traded for Japanese yen, there are similar markets for every pair of traded currencies.

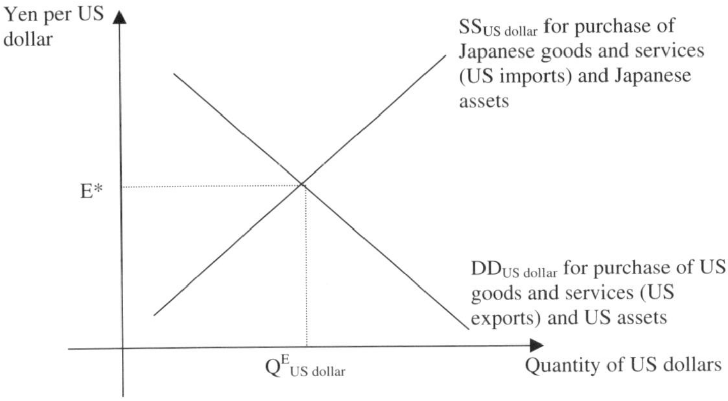

Note: E*-value of the US dollar at equilibrium.

Figure 1. Determination of the US Dollar in the Foreign Exchange Market

The up-ward supply curve for US dollars shows that more US dollars are being supplied in the foreign exchange market as each US dollar exchanges for more yen. The appreciation of the US dollar when the dollar can buy more yen at given prices makes Japanese goods, services and assets cheaper in dollar terms, ceteris paribus. The lower dollar prices resulting from the appreciation of the US dollar induce higher dollar expenditure of Japanese goods, services and assets.

The demand of US dollars in the yen-dollar foreign exchange market is made by anyone who holds yen, mainly Japanese households and firms who want to purchase US goods, services and assets. A Japanese student studying in the US pays his tuition fee in US dollars by offering yen in demand for US dollars. Similarly, a Japanese firm who buys real estate in New York City would demand US dollar to purchase the asset. When the US dollar buys more yen or when the yen buys less US dollars, the US dollar appreciates which makes US goods, services and assets more expensive in terms of yen. Resultantly, Japanese households and firms will demand a lower quantity of US dollars when the US dollar appreciates. Thus, the demand for US dollar is downward sloping as shown in Fig. 1.

As the US maintains a flexible exchange rate regime, the value of the US dollar at equilibrium, E* is determined by the forces of demand and supply in the foreign exchange market. Factors affecting both the demand and supply for US dollars will result in shifts of the respective demand and supply curves causing the equilibrium value of the US dollar to change. Because foreigners buying US goods and services (US exports) and US assets (US capital inflows) affect the demand for US dollars, changes in US exports and US capital inflows lead to shifts in the demand schedule of US dollars. Likewise, Americans buying foreign goods and services (US imports) and foreign assets (US capital outflows) affect the supply of US dollars. Changes in US imports and US capital outflow lead to shifts in the supply schedule of US dollars. Thus, a currency's exchange rate is determined primarily by the nation's international transactions as reflected in the balance of payments account.

INTERNATIONAL CAPITAL FLOWS

Within the balance of payment accounts, the current account records the exports and imports of goods and services and the capital account records purchases and sales of assets, reflecting capital flows. Capital outflow results from domestic residents buying foreign assets and capital inflow results from foreigners buying domestic assets. Within the capital account, international flows of capital can be distinguished as foreign direct investment (FDI) and foreign portfolio investment. Foreign portfolio investment consists of purchases of stocks, also called shares or equities, bonds and bank loans. Using Singapore as an example, if a Singaporean purchases stock in Microsoft Corporation, it is Singapore's foreign portfolio investment. The investment is financed by Singapore. But the business of managing Microsoft Corporation is undertaken by non-Singaporeans. The Singapore stock owner plays a passive role in the business operations of Microsoft Corporation. By contrast, FDI occurs when the residents of one country acquire control of a firm in another country. It may involve buying sufficient stock in an existing firm and along with the owner of the foreign firm becomes a controlling shareholder. This is known as a joint venture FDI. Incidentally, it could involve acquiring complete ownership and control of the foreign firm leading to a merger and acquisition FDI. It could also involve building a new factory or firm from scratch, leading to a greenfield FDI. Development Bank of Singapore (DBS) opening a new branch in Shanghai is an example of Singapore's greenfield FDI in China. In this case, DBS, a firm owned by Singapore is actively managing the investment.

In the examples of foreign investments mentioned above, Singapore residents are buying assets located in another country which results in Singapore's capital outflow. If capital flows are viewed as resources in search of the highest returns, capital from countries where interest rates are low would flow to countries where interest rates are high in order for investment returns to be maximized. Apart from economic and political risks of holding foreign assets and government policies affecting foreign ownership of domestic assets, the real interest returns on holding assets influences the purchase and sale of assets. In the absence of risk, uncertainties and barriers to capital mobility, capital flows occur until interest rates become equal everywhere. In the presence of risk, uncertainties and barriers to capital movement, however, equilibrium flows capital does not require interest rates equality. Differences in interest rates among countries would reflect different risk levels, uncertainties and barriers to capital mobility. Unless changes in interest rates are sufficiently large, capital flows are not likely to occur.

Foreign Direct Investment (FDI)

If interest rate determines capital flows that allow investment returns to be maximized, there are several observations on interest rate returns that distinguish foreign portfolio investment from FDI. Firstly, firms engaging in FDI often finance an important share of the investment in the country where FDI is undertaken. A property developer from Singapore with development projects in China may finance part of the FDI with loans from Chinese banks. If higher interest returns motivate FDI flows, it is hard to understand why FDI firms would finance investments in countries that may not necessarily provide lower cost of loans.

Secondly, foreign portfolio investment and FDI do not behave in similar ways. Increased portfolio investment flows to a certain country may not be accompanied by similar FDI inflows to the same country. In examining the behavior of FDI inflows into countries affected by economic crisis, Lipsey (2001) finds that FDI flows into crisis countries have been more stable than flows of portfolio investment. In the East Asian financial crisis, gross inflows of FDI in the region fell only slightly in 1998 and were back above the previous peak level by 1999. While net inflows of FDI did not fall, net portfolio investment inflows fell sharply which turned into net portfolio outflows.

Thirdly, if interest returns can explain FDI flows, FDI should move to some countries and all industries. On the contrary, FDI is persistently associated with the same industries. In fact, much of the

FDI flows among advanced countries is concentrated in industries intensive in skills and technology such as electronics, chemicals and computer technology and less so in the textile and agricultural industries. This is difficult to account for, if international differences in interest rates are the reason for FDI flows.

Given that interest rate differences is insufficient to explain FDI flows, the academic literature on FDI since the seminal work of Hymer (1960) have focused on profit motives of FDI activities, centered on the ownership of firm-specific assets or knowledge. Appropriating the use of firm-specific assets or knowledge, FDI firms optimize returns and maximize profits, enabling firms to compete effectively in forgein countries. To this end, the demand for FDI is widely viewed as the demand for capital to finance and directly manage business activities in a foreign country. Unlike portfolio investments which do not give investors any controlling interest in the firm's business operations, FDI involves both the ownership and control of the firm's operations. It is this aspect of control that distinguishes foreign portfolio investment from FDI.

When firms locate operations abroad, they face disadvantages not encountered by firms that choose to locate production activities on home ground. These disadvantages include additional efforts in managing geographically widespread operations, dealing with different languages, cultures, product standards and consumer preferences. To overcome these disadvantages, firms with overseas operations must possess firm-specific knowledge or assets. This may be in the form of superior production and management skills. The inventory management strategy used by Toyota, a Japanese automobile manufacturer emphasizing timely arrival of manufacturing parts that result in lower warehousing and associated costs, is an example. In other situation, a foreign firm may place a greater value on a domestic firm than other competitors because the domestic firm offers a potential role in the foreign firm's global strategy. The cross-border acquisition of the marine and mining logistics firm, Sembawang Kimtrans by Toll, a logistics firm headquartered in Australia, is an example. The acquisition FDI was carried out with the aim of expanding Toll's business activities as an integrated logistic provider in Asia. The value of the acquisition to Toll came in the form of firm-specific assets from Sembawang Kimtrans along with sizable market share in the marine, mining and land logistics sector in Indonesia and Singapore. Aside from expanding market share, firms could locate production in a foreign country to appropriate gains from activities there — in research and development, for example. Co and List (2004) show that Japanese FDI in the US is attracted to "knowledge creators", places in the US where there are more research and development activities.

For these reasons, the explanation of FDI in the academic literature has focused on the industrial organization of firms. Interest returns and costs as factors that motivate FDI to the extent that they may be right, do not seem to explain FDI flows better than the industrial organization approach, at least among industrial nations. This includes the depreciation of a country's exchange rate that incidentally results in a lower cost of investment. The possibility of a relationship of exchange rate depreciation that could lead to more capital inflows does not seem to be supported by economic reasoning. This is because, returns on risk-adjusted assets traded in a world with increasingly less barriers to capital mobility are expected to be equalized. In the context of FDI, when the foreign currency depreciates, the profits generated by foreign operations and expressed in terms of the home country's currency will also decrease. Even as it implies that the cost of establishing operations in the foreign country is lower with the depreciation of the foreign currency, it really makes no difference where and how a firm finances FDI since firms have access to the same international capital market. If the US dollar depreciates, the US becomes a cheaper place for any firm to produce. Hence, there are no "bargains" with the depreciation of exchange rate.

EXCHANGE RATE AND FDI

Despite the appealing argument, data on inflows of FDI in the US show a systematic relationship with the US dollar. Since 1973, after the Bretton woods fixed exchange rate regime, the depreciation of the US dollar shows a positive correlation with FDI inflows in the

US. The explanation of the correlation between the value of a currency and FDI inflows is addressed by Froot and Stein (1991). They identify information asymmetry between lenders and borrowers and build on the idea that FDI firms face a higher cost of financing when they borrow from external sources than when they use internally generated funds. This is because borrowers know more about the use of borrowed funds in generating returns from FDI projects than lenders. Lenders who have less information on how their loans are utilized must gather information. In collecting information to monitor the performance of loans and the payoffs of investment projects, they incur monitoring costs. The cost of acquiring information drives a wedge between the cost of financing FDI projects from external sources such as bank loans, bonds and stock issues; and the cost of financing FDI projects from internal sources such as retained profits. The more internal funds rather than external funds, a firm uses to finance FDI projects, the lower will be the firm's total cost of capital. It also implies that the more net wealth a firm brings into its FDI projects, the lower will be its total cost of capital.

Given the link between wealth position of firms and investment opportunities, Froot and Stein (1991) develop the explanation for the persistent relationship between exchange rates and FDI. Using the US as the home country, they explain that foreigners will hold more of their wealth denominated in their respective countries' currencies. A depreciation of the US dollar increases the relative wealth of foreign firms and therefore lower their relative cost of capital. The relative wealth increase resulting from the depreciation of the US dollar enables foreign firms to bid higher for US assets.

The explanation can be illustrated with an example. Suppose a Singapore firm and a US firm are bidding to purchase an office building in New York City. Either firm can obtain a loan from a bank on the same terms. The bank will lend at an interest rate of 10% for up to 90% of the purchase price. The US firm has 7 million US dollars (USD) and Singapore firm has 10 million Singapore dollars (SGD) and the exchange rate prevails at 1.5 SGD/USD. In this scenario, the US firm can make a USD 7 million down payment and can bid as high as USD 70 million for the building. The Singapore firm on the contrary has wealth of only USD 6.67 million and can bid only as high as USD 67.7 million. The US firm wins the bidding in this case. Suppose the US dollar depreciates to an exchange rate of 1.2 SGD/USD. The wealth of the Singapore firm now increases to USD 8.33 million and given the US dollar depreciation, wins the bidding. The resulting US dollar depreciation that increased the relative wealth of the Singaporean firm and changed the outcome of the bidding.

In the example above, the imperfection in capital markets is a result of asymmetric information. Capital remains perfectly mobile because the Singapore firm and the US firm have access to the same external borrowing facilities. It is information asymmetry that drives the imperfection and this imperfection affects only information intensive investments. Investments which are not intensive in information such as portfolio investments in stocks and bonds are unlikely to be influenced by imperfect capital markets caused by asymmetric information. Empirical tests in Froot and Stein (1991) show evidence that the value of the US dollar influences only US FDI inflows. Portfolio investment inflows consisting of stocks and corporate bonds do not show any significant statistical relationship with the value of the US dollar. Further empirical evidence of the relationship between foreign exchange rates and FDI inflows are found in Klein and Rosengren (1994), Klein, Peek and Rosengren (2002) and Alba, Wang and Ho (2007).

An alternative explanation for the correlation between FDI and the real exchange rate is developed in Blonigen (1997). Instead of assuming imperfect capital markets, Blonigen (1997) assumes imperfect goods markets. If the goods markets are segmented, with US firms having limited access to foreign markets, foreign firms that can extend operations abroad will value more highly firm-specific assets in the US when the US dollar depreciates.

The acquisition of US firm-specific assets, namely advance technology and superior management techniques allows foreign firms to generate returns in foreign markets which are relatively inaccessible by US firms. The market access asymmetry implies that a depreciation of the US dollar will induce more acquisition of US firm-specific assets in the US as foreign firms will place higher values on these assets. The key assumption in the explanation proposed by Blonigen (1997) is the asymmetric access to the goods markets between domestic and foreign firms. The foreign acquisition of US firm-specific assets generates returns for foreign firms in foreign markets that US firms have limited access. In this regard, Blonigen (1997) identifies the Japanese market which is widely known to be insulated to some degree from foreign import penetration and FDI. While the opportunity to purchase US firm-specific assets remain the same for the US firm and the Japanese firm, both firms face different opportunities to generate returns when the US firm has limited access to the Japanese market. As a result, the depreciation of the US dollar raises the valuation of US firm-specific assets by Japanese firms while the valuation of US assets by US firms remains unchanged.

In 1989, Sony, a Japanese electronics manufacturer acquired film-making technology when Sony bought Columbia Pictures, a US firm. The acquisition provided Sony, which was predominantly an electronics manufacturer at that time, with film-production technology and firm-specific assets, enabling the company, to enter and operate in the film making industry. The merger and acquisition resulting in the formation of Sony Pictures continued to produce movies which are screened not only in the US but also in Japan, where it could have been less accessible, had the acquisition FDI not taken place.

CONCLUSION

This chapter presents selected developments in the FDI literature on the role of exchange rate in attracting FDI inflows. The explanations developed in Froot and Stein (1991) and Blonigen (1997) are not mutually exclusive as they draw on different perspectives of FDI. Froot and Stein (1991) assume imperfect capital markets due to information asymmetry between lenders and borrowers while Blonigen (1997) assumes imperfect goods market because of market access asymmetry between domestic and foreign firms. In both explanations of FDI, assumptions underlying economic theories eased to accommodate market imperfections in order to resolve differences in empirical observations and economic theory.

END NOTES

Alba, JD, P Wang, WY Ho (2007). Relative access to credit, relative wealth and FDI: Firm-level evidence from Japanese FDI into the United States. *Journal of Economic Integration*, 22, pp. 231-255.

Blonigen, BA (1997). Firm-specific assets and the link between exchange rates and foreign direct investment. *American Economic Review*, 87, pp. 447-465.

Caves, RE (1989). Exchange rate movements and foreign direct investment in the United States. In *The Internationalization of the US Markets*, Audretsch, DB and MP Claudon (eds.), 199-228. New York: New York University Press.

Co, CY and JA List (2004). Is foreign direct investment attracted to 'knowledge creators'? *Applied Economics*, 36, pp. 1143-1149.

Frank, RH and BS Bernanke (2007). *Principles of Economics*, 3rd Ed., McGraw-Hill.

Froot, KA and JC Stein (1991). Exchange rates and foreign direct investment: An imperfect capital markets approach. *Quarterly Journal of Economics*, 106, pp. 1191-1217.

Graham, EM and PR Krugman (1995). *Foreign Direct Investment in the United States*. Washington, DC: Institute for International Economics.

Hymer, SH (1960). *The International Operations of National Firms: A Study of Direct Foreign Investment*. PhD dissertation, MIT.

Klein, MW and ES Rosengren (1994). The real exchange rate and foreign direct investment in the United States: Relative wealth vs. Relative wage effects. *Journal of International Economics*, 36, pp. 373-389.

Klein, MW, J Peek and ES Rosengren (2002). Troubled banks, impaired foreign direct investment: The role of relative access to credit. *American Economic Review*, 92, pp. 664-682.

Lipsey, RE (2001). Foreign Direct Investors in Three Financial Crises, *NBER Working Paper* No. 8084.

Mankiw, NG (2007). *Principles of Economics*, 4th Ed., Thomson-South Western.

Index